Bitcoin Revolution - The Rise of the New Monetary Standard

The Amazing Guide to Master the World of Cryptocurrency and Blockchain - Learn the Only Profitable Bitcoin Investing Strategy

By Frederick Patton

The following Book is reproduced below with the goal of providing information that is as accurate and reliable as possible. Regardless, purchasing this Book can be seen as consent to the fact that both the publisher and the author of this book are in no way experts on the topics discussed within and that any recommendations or suggestions that are made herein are for entertainment purposes only. Professionals should be consulted as needed prior to undertaking any of the action endorsed herein. This declaration is deemed fair and valid by both the American Bar Association and the Committee of Publishers Association and is legally binding throughout the United States. Furthermore, the transmission, duplication, or reproduction of any of the following work including specific information will be considered an illegal act irrespective of if it is done electronically or in print. This extends to creating a secondary or tertiary copy of the work or a recorded copy and is only allowed with the express written consent from the Publisher. All additional rights reserved. The information in the following pages is broadly considered a truthful and accurate account of facts and as such, any inattention, use, or misuse of the information in question by the reader will render any resulting actions solely under their purview. There are no scenarios in which the publisher or the original author of this work can be in any fashion deemed liable for any hardship or damages that may befall them after undertaking information described herein.

Additionally, the information in the following pages is intended only for informational purposes and should thus be thought of as universal. As befitting its nature, it is presented without assurance regarding its prolonged validity or interim quality. Trademarks that are mentioned are done without written consent and can in no way be considered an endorsement from the trademark holder.

Table of Contents

Introduction

Bitcoin has taken the world by storm once again when it crossed $20,000 per BTC in December of last year. After more than 2 years of bear market, the most famous cryptocurrency surpassed its previous all time high.

A lot of people are now trying to improvise themselves as professional investors and are losing a lot of money, only helping those who actually know what they are doing accumulate an incredible amount of wealth that will lead to generational fortunes.

To join the club of the few investors that actually make it, you need the right strategies and the right mindset. Notice how we did not include a large initial capital. In fact, while having more money to trade with means having more fire power, it is not necessary to have thousands of dollars to accumulate Bitcoin and build wealth.

In fact, when we started investing in Bitcoin we only had a few hundreds to put into the market, but that sum yielded us thousands and thousands of dollars over the span of a few years.

In this book you are going to discover all the strategies that have allowed us to take investing skills to the next level and everything that helped us understand Bitcoin. If you diligently apply our advice, we are sure you are going to see amazing results in a relative short period of time, since this bull run is offering an amazing number of opportunities.

Please, stay away from all the shiny objects of the cryptocurrency world. Just focus on Bitcoin, study it deeply and then milk it like a cash cow!

To your success!

Chapter 1

What is Bitcoin?

Bitcoin (₿, BTC, XBT) is a cryptocurrency otherwise called cryptographic currency. In the case of the unitary denomination, it is written "bitcoin" and, in the case of the peer-to-peer payment system, it is written "Bitcoin". The idea was first presented in November 2008 by one person, or a group of people, under the pseudonym Satoshi Nakamoto. The source code for the implementation of Bitcoin was released in 2009.

The G20 considers Bitcoin to be a “crypto-asset”. The term “crypto-asset” refers to “virtual assets stored on an electronic wallet allowing a community of users accepting them in payment to carry out transactions without having to resort to legal tender”.

Operation

To create and manage bitcoins, Bitcoin relies on software. In this software, bitcoins are created according to a protocol that pays the agents (called "miners") who have processed transactions. These agents use their computing power to verify, secure and record the transactions in a virtual ledger called the blockchain. The word blockchain comes from the fact that the basic entity of Bitcoin is called a block, and that the blocks are then connected in a chain.

For each new block accepted, the verification-security-recording activity, called mining, is remunerated by newly created bitcoins and by the costs of the transactions processed. As a currency or a commodity, bitcoin can be exchanged for other currencies or commodities, goods or services. The cryptocurrency exchange rate is set on specialized marketplaces and fluctuates according to the law of supply and demand.

It is possible to buy bitcoins online on specialized platforms, physical terminals or in exchange for any good or service with a person who already has them (the transaction can be done from smartphone to smartphone). The platforms also make it possible to follow in real time the evolution of the price of bitcoin compared to other currencies or cryptocurrencies.

Account unit

Bitcoin's unit of account is bitcoin. Its emission is limited to 20,999,999.977 units, each divisible to the eighth decimal place (called Satoshi or Sat). The official currency symbol was registered and accepted in 2015 with Unicode. The corresponding acronyms, used by the exchange platforms, are BTC and XBT. Among the unofficial symbols used are ฿ and Ƀ.

Decentralization

The system operates without a central authority or a single administrator. It is managed in a decentralized manner thanks to the consensus of all the nodes of the network. Bitcoin is the largest decentralized crypto currency, with a capitalization of over one trillion dollars as of April 5th, 2021 ($ 130 billion as of January 1st, 2020).

Means of payment

As a means of payment, bitcoin is accepted by a growing number of merchants, encouraged by transaction fees generally lower than the 2 to 3% charged by credit card organizations and independent of the amount of the financial transaction. However, in 2017 the fees increased dramatically over the course of a few months, from $0.2 in 2016 to $20 on certain days in December 2017, so that the Steam platform or Microsoft withdrew Bitcoin as a payment method, precisely because of too high transaction fees (Microsoft again authorized Bitcoin in January 2018).

In order to address the issue of excessively high transaction fees, the gradual rollout of various technology enhancements (Segwit, Lightning Network, batch transactions, Schnorr) throughout 2018 and 2019 allowed fees to drop to around $0.05 for non-urgent transactions, and even amounts less than $ 0.0001 for Lightning type transactions. Unlike credit cards, any charges are borne not by the seller but by the buyer, who chooses to pay them voluntarily. A bitcoin transaction is irrevocable and cannot be reversed. Despite a 500% growth in the number of merchants accepting bitcoin in 2014, the cryptocurrency is not very established in the retail trade, but continues to gain a foothold in trade.

Use

Between January 2009 and March 2010, using bitcoin was a hobby among crypto enthusiasts, and bitcoin had no real value. However, in April 2010, bitcoin started trading in an exchange for $0.003, and soon after, in May 2010, it was already worth $0.01. A few months later, in July 2010, 0.08 dollars were added to its value again. These numbers reflect the rapid rise in prices that this zero-value cryptocurrency has experienced at 10 cents.

Since its creation in 2009 and until the closure by the American authorities of Silk Road in 2013, bitcoin was used mainly as a medium of exchange by criminal networks for gambling, the purchase of illicit substances, or for hacked databases. The cryptocurrency has attracted the attention of financial authorities, legislative bodies in various countries, particularly the United States, and the mainstream media.

Nevertheless, in recent years, cryptocurrency has matured and a growing number of studies conclude that these illegal activities, although they still exist as in any payment system, only involve a minority share of cryptocurrency exchanges. The United States Senate also recognizes that bitcoin makes it possible to provide perfectly legitimate financial services.

Safe store of value

According to some of the experts, bitcoin would be a safe haven much more than a means of payment, even if unlike gold, Bitcoin can indeed be used for these two purposes. Conversely, other financial experts consider Bitcoin to be far too volatile to be a safe haven, but it has only existed since 2009 and its possible safe haven status will only be possible after a first period of intense volatility . As for the question of whether Bitcoin can reach the market value of gold (or even exceed it), this remains much debated. However, it should be noted that with its trillion dollars evaluation, Bitcoin is not too far from reaching the value of Silver, which is approximately 1.4 trillion dollars.

Chapter 2

The History of Bitcoin

Bitcoin is an improvement on the concept of b-money, imagined by Wei Dai in 1999, and bitgold, described in 2005 by Nick Szabo. Bitcoin in particular solves the crucial problem of the trust model: servers considered serious vote with their computing power to determine the legitimate transaction chain. In b-money, the servers were supposed to pay a security deposit according to a not very explicit mechanism. The idea of using a computational proof chain was put forward in the bitgold project although Nick Szabo only proposed to use a majority of addresses to establish the legitimacy of a chain of transactions, which left the problem of controlling the number of addresses.

Satoshi Nakamoto claimed that he worked on bitcoin from 2007 to 2009. As early as 2008, he posted a document on a mailing list describing the digital currency. In February 2009, he published an announcement about his work on the P2P Foundation site. On January 3, 2009, the first block or genesis block was created. In February 2009, he distributed the first version of the Bitcoin software on the P2P Foundation site and to operate the network, he used his computer and thus generated the first bitcoins. Along with other developers, Nakamoto continued the implementation of the software and its Bitcoin-Qt version until 2010.

Developers and the bitcoin community gradually lost contact with him in the middle of 2010. On December 12, 2010, a final message was posted by Nakamoto on the main forum. Shortly before disappearing, Nakamoto designates Gavin Andresen as his successor by giving him access to the SourceForge bitcoin project and a copy of the alert key. The latter is a unique private cryptographic key allowing to mitigate the effects of a potential attack on the Bitcoin system, such as the discovery of a cryptographic flaw allowing to modify the transactions, or the take of control of more than 51% of the nodes in the network. During an alert, the operators of the nodes of the network can either warn their users or stop recording transactions.

On September 27, 2012, the Bitcoin Foundation was created. Important characters from the world of new technologies quickly supported the project, such as Wences Casares.

The identity of Satoshi Nakamoto

Several people claimed to be Satoshi Nakamoto, but none of them could prove it. There is no trace of his identity before the creation of Bitcoin. On his profile, Satoshi claimed to be a 40-year-old Japanese.

In March 2014, journalist Leah McGrath Goodman from Newsweek magazine announced that she had tracked down the inventor of Bitcoin who she said would be a 64-year-old Japanese-American whose birth name is "Satoshi Nakamoto", although he changed his name to "Dorian Prentice Satoshi

Nakamoto" at the age of 23. He is believed to be a retired physicist living in California. This thesis was methodically dismantled a month later by linguists from Aston University in England who carried out an in-depth study of the linguistic correspondences between the written productions of the author of the Bitcoin white paper and several suspected personalities, notably Dorian Nakamoto.

In 2016, Craig Steven Wright, an Australian entrepreneur, claimed to be Satoshi Nakamoto. However, strong doubts remain.

Adoption

The history of Bitcoin adoption is quite remarkable, as it has been a long process of fake bans and unjustified threats to the cryptocurrency space. In the following pages we are going to track back the adoption process of Bitcoin, starting from 2012. Here are the main milestones of BTC adoption.

- On November 16th, 2012, WordPress started accepting bitcoins for its paid services.

- On November 28th, 2012, the remuneration of miners decreased for the first time, from 50 to 25 BTC. The bitcoin source code provides for a halving of the remuneration every two hundred and ten thousand blocks mined, or approximately every four years.

- On December 6th, 2012, a partnership between the startup Paymium (French exchange site) and the company Aqoba (payment institution) enabled Paymium to operate as a payment service provider, and therefore to keep accounts in euros and issue payment cards usable in euros and bitcoins. On February 14th, 2013, the Reddit community site set up a system to buy "Reddit Gold" with bitcoins.

- On February 16th, 2013, the online storage site Mega, successor to Megaupload, started accepting payments in bitcoin. On October 14th, 2013, the giant Baidu (Chinese equivalent of Google) started accepting bitcoin transactions for its Jiasule firewall service.

- On October 29th, 2013, the first automatic bitcoin cash dispenser-exchanger went into service in Vancouver. In September 2016, more than seven hundred and seventy of these automatic distributor-exchangers were installed worldwide, including four in France.

- On November 21st, 2013, the University of Nicosia announced that it accepted bitcoin and opened a master's degree in economics specializing in digital currencies. On November 22nd, 2013, Richard Branson announced that Virgin Galactic was going to accept bitcoins as a means of payment for its space tourism flights.

- On November 29th, 2013, Jiangsu Telecom (third largest Chinese operator), a subsidiary of China Telecom, started accepting bitcoins.

- On March 25th, 2014, the US tax authorities declared that bitcoin should not be considered as a currency, but as a commodity, whose transactions are subject to taxation on capital gains. This involves taking into account the exchange rate at which a bitcoin has been acquired and the one at which it is used in order to calculate the realized gain, which makes the legal use of bitcoin in the United States particularly difficult.

- On May 9th, 2014, the United States Election Commission accepted that election campaigns could be funded in bitcoins up to a limit of $100 per election cycle.

- On September 23rd, 2014, Paypal allowed certain North American digital goods merchants selected by partner bitcoin payment processors to accept payments in bitcoins, and thus very gradually opened up to bitcoin. As of October 16th, 2017, there were Bitcoin ATMs around the world.

- In December 2017, the French Minister of Public Accounts, Gérald Darmanin, reminded

French taxpayers of the requirement to declare income, when it comes to capital gains realized during bitcoin transactions.

- In November 2018, the Ohio government announced that it was accepting Bitcoin tax payments. In January 2020, an investing.com study revealed that 9% of financial advisers already put part of their client's funds in bitcoin to protect them from monetary troubles.

Important moments

During the adoption phase there have been quite a few important moments that changed the course of Bitcoin's life. Here are the most important ones.

- On August 15th, 2010, a block was generated containing a transaction creating 184,467,440,737 bitcoins for three different addresses. This flaw is linked to the fact that the code did not foresee the case of creating such large amounts of bitcoins. This problem was solved automatically by the bitcoin blockchain and these bitcoins no longer exist.

- On March 12th, 2013, an incident occurred related to the non-backward compatibility of version 0.8.0: the chain split into several versions and some remained blocked for a few hours. After a few moments of panic, the system was able to correct itself, signaling the strength of the blockchain technology.

- On April 11th, 2013, the value of bitcoin collapsed from $266 to $105 before stabilizing at $160 in less than six hours. On April 13th, the price reached $66. This massive drop occurred after a big bull run, where the price of Bitcoin rose six times in just a few weeks. For those that are already familiar with Bitcoin's price action, we are sure they are smiling just by thinking about such low prices.

- On October 2nd, 2013, Ross Ulbricht was arrested. He was the alleged founder of Silk Road, which was shut down by the FBI and used only bitcoin for all of its transactions. More on that in a dedicated chapter.

- On February 11th, 2014, the Bitcoin network was the victim of a massive and concerted attack launched on numerous exchange platforms, where quite a few bitcoins were stolen. This was just the preview of what was going to happen a few days later. In fact, on February 24th, 2014, the Mt. Gox trading platform suffered a record loss of 744,408 BTC, the equivalent of more than 44 billion dollars. The site was closed shortly after. A crisis management document has been drawn up and is publicly available on its website, we suggest you check it out because it is quite interesting (https://www.mtgox.com/). Due to this incident, bitcoin lost more than 38% of its value in the first quarter of 2014. On September 11th, 2015, Mark Karpelès, owner of the Mt. Gox platform was indicted in Japan for embezzlement. He is suspected of having embezzled 2.3 million dollars of bitcoin deposits.

- In May 2016, the Gatecoin exchange site was hacked and had 250 bitcoins and 185,000 ether stolen. The hacker managed to bypass the online storage limits of the exchange platform's assets: while only 5% of the deposits are not cold stored, the hacker managed to empty these deposits while continuing to feed the address by transfer of cold storage assets from the exchange platform. After this event, almost every trading and exchanging platform decided to implement a new protection mechanism, in order to improve their safety.

- On August 3rd, 2016, the Bitfinex exchange site reported the theft of 119,756 bitcoins on its exchange platform, which at the time counted for around $65 million.

- On May 7th, 2019, hackers stole more than 7,000 Bitcoins from the Binance Cryptocurrency Exchange, worth over US $40 million. Binance CEO Zhao Changpeng said, "Hackers used a variety of techniques, including phishing, viruses and other attacks. They had

> the patience to wait and perform well orchestrated actions through multiple independent accounts at the most opportune moment". It was this event that inspired Binance to improve its protection mechanism even further.

All incidents related to exchange platforms only affect people who do not themselves hold the private keys of their bitcoin wallet. Not your keys, not your bitcoins as they say. As you can see, every time the Bitcoin network has been attacked, new solutions were found to make sure the same issue would not happen in the future. In our opinion, this is one of the main strengths in this system. In fact, since it is developed by people, it can easily adapt to new hacking methods and attacks. It is pretty interesting to see the evolution of Bitcoin and if you want to actually invest in it safely, you need to know a bit of its history as well.

A common hacking technique

The technique known as the Trojan Horse makes it possible to change the address of the recipient of the cryptocurrency transaction. CryptoShuffler is one of the software using this technique. This rare technique has little effect because it suffices for the payment sender to visually check the first/last characters of the destination address to make sure that it is not being fooled.

Price evolution against the dollar

When it was created in February 2009, the cryptocurrency was initially traded only as an experiment by a few rare users and its value was zero. On October 12th, 2009, the first known bitcoin sale took place, where two users traded 5,050 bitcoins for $5.02 using a Paypal transfer, which equates to a price of around $0.001 per bitcoin.

In March 2010, Bitcoinmarket.com was the first bitcoin exchange platform to be opened, thus allowing continuous quotation of the price of bitcoin. It was the beginning of an era and every Bitcoin enthusiast should be thankful to this website for what it has done for the community.

On February 9th, 2011, bitcoin reached the valuation of one full dollar. On November 29th, 2013, the value of a bitcoin exceeded that of an ounce of gold, to nearly $1,250. Once again, for those that are familiar with today price action, these numbers do not seem so incredible. However, if you think about it, we are talking about a huge price development in just a couple of years. What other asset did over 1000% in just two years? The answer is very simple: no other asset managed to do it.

Bitcoin, mainly traded for yuan and dollars, can also be traded for euros on a dozen platforms. Until November 2013, Mt. Gox was the most important of these platforms in terms of transaction volume (~ 70%) and the practice had been taken to consider its price as representative of the market. As a result of the problems encountered, users turned away from it, causing the price of bitcoin to drop sharply on Mt.

Gox, with prices observed on other platforms only slightly affected.

The price experienced a 400% increase between January and March 2013, before correcting itself severely on April 10th, following a failure of the Mt. Gox exchange site and probable panic sales. The price fell back to the level of the previous month, around $50. Between December 4th and 5th, 2013, following a warning from the People's Bank of China and the Bank of France, the price lost nearly 35% in 24 hours.

On February 19th, 2014, the price collapsed following the announcement of the disappearance of 850,000 bitcoins on Mt. Gox. On this exchange platform, bitcoin goes from $185, on February 18, to $73 24 hours later, while it remains close to $400 on other platforms. Mt.Gox declared bankruptcy on February 28, 2014. On May 1st, 2014, a group of investors by the name of Sunlot Holdings offered to buy the site for one symbolic bitcoin.

In 2016, after the Brexit announcement on June 24th, the value of bitcoin skyrocketed, gaining more than

9%, while all financial centers plunged for more than a week. This was probably the first time that the true strength of Bitcoin was shown to the world. In fact, BTC is an asset that does particularly well when there is turbulence in the world. We have seen this in 2020, where it rose by over 600% in just one year.

In 2017, Bitcoin topped out at around $19,000 and entered a long bear market of over 2 years. Those who accumulated during that time were brave enough to survive more than 700 days without seeing the asset climbing back to its all time high. However, in 2020, Bitcoin finally managed to break that level and skyrocketed. At the time of writing this book, one bitcoin is worth around $60,000.

Think about it, if you bought $10 worth of Bitcoin on February 9th, 2011, you would now have an equivalent of over $600,000. These kind of numbers really impress us.

Chapter 3

The Idea behind Bitcoin

Bitcoin's theoretical roots lie in the Austrian school of economics and its critique of the current monetary system and interventions by governments and other entities, which this school of thought says exacerbates business cycles and massive inflation.

One of the topics that the Austrian School of Economics, led by Eugen von Böhm-Bawerk, Ludwig von Mises and Friedrich A. Hayek, focused on is the business cycle. In fact, according to the Austrian theory, business cycles are the consequence of inevitable monetary interventions in the market, whereby an excessive expansion of bank credit leads to an increase in the stock of bank credit in a fractional reserve system, which in turn leads to artificially low interest rates.

In this situation, entrepreneurs, guided by distorted interest rate signals, embark on over-ambitious investment projects that do not match the preferences of consumers at that time for intertemporal consumption (that is, i.e. their short-term decisions and future consumption). Sooner or later, this generalized imbalance can no longer last and leads to a recession, during which companies must liquidate failed investment projects and restructure their production structures according to the intertemporal preferences of consumers. As a result, many economists in Austrian schools are calling for the abandonment of this process by abolishing the fractional reserve banking system and reverting to a currency based on the gold standard, which cannot be easily manipulated by authorities.

A related area in which Austrian economists have been very active is monetary theory. Friedrich A. Hayek is one of the best known names in this field. He wrote some very influential publications, such as

Denationalization of Money (1976), in which he postulated that governments should not have a monopoly on issuing money. On the contrary, he suggests that private banks should be allowed to issue non-interest bearing certificates, based on their own trademarks. These certificates (i.e. currencies) should be open to competition and would be traded at varying exchange rates. Any currency that can guarantee stable purchasing power would eliminate other less stable currencies from the market. The result of this process of competition and profit maximization would be a highly efficient monetary system in which only stable currencies would coexist.

The following ideas are generally shared by Bitcoin supporters.

- They see Bitcoin as a good starting point to end the monopoly of central banks in issuing money.

- They strongly criticize the current fractional reserve banking system, which allows banks to extend their credit supply beyond their actual reserves and, at the same time, allows depositors to withdraw their funds to their checking accounts at any time.

Specificity of Bitcoin

We must distinguish between bitcoin, cryptocurrency and on the other hand Bitcoin, the payment system in this currency. In these two aspects, Bitcoin differs from pre-existing systems on some important points.

First of all, unlike other monetary currencies, Bitcoin is not the embodiment of the authority of any state, bank, or business. The value of bitcoin is determined in a fully floating fashion by the economic use that is made of it and by the foreign exchange market. The rules organizing the monetary issue are determined solely by the free computer code of the Bitcoin software.

Furthermore, as a payment system, Bitcoin is distinguished by the fact that its operation does not require the use of a centralized infrastructure keeping accounts of the amounts held in order to ensure transactions. The role of guarantee and verification exists, but is assigned approximately every ten minutes to a computer of the network chosen at random according to its power.

Bitcoin is based on a cryptographic protocol whose main purpose is, on the one hand, to resolve the so-called double payment problem, which had hitherto prevented the emergence of such a type of currency, and, on the other hand, to "prohibit" the falsification of stakeholder identifiers and the value of bitcoin stock in electronic wallets identified by a given address.

Monetary principles behind Bitcoin

From a monetary point of view, bitcoin is distinguished from other currencies by the major fact that the monetary aggregate is not designed to adapt to the production of wealth.

The total amount and the emission rate of the units are entered explicitly in the computer code of the software, according to a mathematical rule of the geometric series type. Bitcoins are issued slowly and steadily, decreasingly, reaching a maximum amount of 21 million around the year 2140.

All fiat currencies experience inflation, from low to high depending on the policies of their central bank. Conversely, bitcoin currency is likely to end up experiencing deflation, as the maximum amount of bitcoins that can be created is set in the software in advance at 21 million. In addition to this, bitcoins lost by users will never be replaced. This is why the Bitcoin project is considered by the community of its creators as an original experiment in economic terms, constituting a kind of test of the monetary theses of the Austrian school of economics. In fact, Friedrich Hayek, Nobel laureate in economics, in 1976 called for the reestablishment of monetary free will in his book "For a true competition of currencies". The success or failure of Bitcoin is difficult to predict, but it is impossible to say it has not done well so far.

Scalability of the protocol

On July 14th, 2010, shortly after the launch of the Bitcoin system, Satoshi Nakamoto created a limit of 1MB for each newly created block every ten minutes on the bitcoin blockchain.

At that time, transactions were free because few in number, and developers had a legitimate concern that attackers could "spam" the transaction network, arbitrarily creating huge blocks and permanently inflating the size of the blockchain. This limit was intended to prevent this kind of attack until a better solution could be put in place. Satoshi Nakamoto had proposed a solution that would involve increasing the block size to certain block heights, effectively increasing the limit to a predetermined rate similar to how new bitcoins are issued.

The scalability of the Bitcoin system has been a constant source of debate in the community since the introduction of this block size limit. This 1 MB limit, initially thought to limit the number of transactions per second to seven, posed no problem at a time when the actual number of transactions hardly exceeded 2.3 transactions per second (2010). So, seven transactions per second was three times the volume of bitcoin's busiest day at that time, leaving developers years to find a better solution. In addition to this, the protocol provided for the introduction of transaction fees over time, which would make this type of attack more costly and ineffective.

Saturation of transaction integration capacity

From 2014, the success of the Bitcoin system led to a continuous rise in the number of transactions which eventually hit the 1MB limit in 2016. A developer, Gavin Andresen, initially proposed 20MB blocks, but the increase was deemed too aggressive by the community. Another proposal, BIP10191, offered to increase the block size by 40% per year from 8MB which led to the creation of a new cryptocurrency, different from bitcoin, called Bitcoin XT92. Other proposals have been made like BIP10093 with a 2MB block which leads to the Bitcoin Classic cryptocurrency and more aggressive "emerging consensus" approaches that allow users to "vote" on the best block size at a time given through Bitcoin Unlimited.

Other members of the community preferred not to favor an increase in the block size, but to change the protocol itself so that more transactions are integrated in a block by reducing their size or increasing the creation frequency of new blocks.

When the number of transactions eventually reached the block size limit, the pool of pending transactions became full. The only way to get a given transaction into the blockchain faster for a user was to increase transaction fees, which reached nearly $5 at the end of 2016. This made Bitcoin uncompetitive against existing services like Western Union or Paypal on the strict basis of speed and cost.

The New York Agreement

The stalled debate on scalability weakened the Bitcoin Core system and led to the growing success of the vote in favor of the Bitcoin Unlimited movement, especially among miners, in large part due to frustration at the lack of upgrading solutions. The approach of the development team, called segwit (segregated witness), of not increasing the block size limit, but differently partitioning the digital signatures of transactions into "extension block", was not working to achieve sufficient consensus.

A compromise was found in an industry consensus in 2017 called Segwit2x97, which combined the segregated witness proposal with a block size increase to 2MB. This proposal was implemented on August 1st, 2017 for segregated witnesses and the block size increase came into effect in November 2017 at block 494,784. It was a major update to the Bitcoin system.

Nonetheless, the scalability debate was still heated and a breakaway group unilaterally increased the block size to 8MB while rejecting the Segwit proposal on August 1, 2017. This decision led to the emergence of a new cryptocurrency, called Bitcoin Cash.

Bitcoin XT (created in August 2015), Bitcoin Unlimited (created in January 2016), Bitcoin Classic (created in February 2016 before being discontinued in November 2017), Bitcoin Cash (created in August 2017) and Bitcoin Gold (created in October 2017) are alternative cryptocurrencies to Bitcoin (also called Bitcoin Core) that try to solve the problem of transaction fees.

Distribution of wealth

Bitcoins are concentrated in the hands of a few whales. The distribution of "wealth" is such that 2,100 addresses hold 40.2% of the total. However this kind of information is not very useful because some of these addresses are dead (keys lost when a unit of bitcoin was not worth 1 cent). Our opinion is that now that we are seeing institutions jumping on board, we will have much more concentration in terms of the number of bitcoins owned by whales. As the price rises, it will be more and more difficult for the average Joe to have ownership of one full bitcoin.

Chapter 4

How Bitcoin Works

Bitcoin does not have an independent existence of the Bitcoin payment system which allows transactions to be made from one account to another, thanks to software called wallets, and the authority being ensured by software from verification called miners. The data of all transactions constitute a public ledger under private law called "blockchain" because of its structure, and an agent uses bitcoins by recording their transactions in the Bitcoin system's blockchain.

The Bitcoin system is computer-based. In other words, the Bitcoin system resides on the Internet. Downloading and installing the appropriate software allows you to become a Bitcoin user by interacting with hardware of your choice, including a smartphone or computer. To pay or be paid in bitcoin, the user must connect to the system. This connection offers two functions: the creation of any number of accounts, and the ease of carrying out transactions consisting of the transfer of bitcoins from an own account to the account of a third party.

The essential function of the Bitcoin system lies in the transactions which are subjected to a validity check by the competent computers and are irrevocably entered in a public register. This public ledger or blockchain can be viewed anywhere by anyone, as long as they have an internet connection. During the consultation no alteration is possible.

Bitcoin transaction mechanism

A Bitcoin transaction requires two fundamental steps. First, dedicated network nodes (the "miners") create a new block by grouping together recently completed transactions and adding a header to them containing the date and time, a checksum ("hash "), which will also serve as the unique identifier of the block, and the identifier of the previous block.

Secondly, after having checked the validity of all the transactions contained in this new block and their consistency with the transactions already recorded, each miner adds it to their local version of the register (or chain of blocks).
The public register is copied several times. The complete history of all transactions can then be read by viewing all nodes in the network that manage a copy of the blockchain. The copy can reveal possible differences between files, in the event of disagreement. In this case, any differences between these copies must be resolved by the software.

If you think about it, transactions consist of debiting certain accounts in order to credit others.

They are made up of inputs and outputs. Each output includes an amount and the public key of the credited address, or more generally a program (a script) making it possible to authorize or not the transfer of the amount of this output to another transaction. Each input designates an output from a previous transaction and has a program (script) that provides the data expected by the script appearing in that output. The sum of the values of the outputs must be less than or equal to the sum of the values of the inputs. The difference constitutes the miner's remuneration.

When creating a transaction, scripts for each entry are executed; first the script of the entry itself, then the script of the earlier exit that the entry refers to. The transaction is only committed if the result is "true" for all inputs.

These scripts are written in an internal language designed by Nakamoto. This language is intentionally minimalist and not Turing-complete in order to prevent the system from being able to engage in infinite loops. The use of scripts should allow the software to easily adapt to future developments and allow support for advanced features such as transactions involving multiple signatures or smart contracts.

Transactions made by a node are broadcast to its neighbors. These validate the transactions they receive and gradually consolidate them into a local pool before passing them on to their own neighbors. The valid transactions are thus broadcast step by step to all the nodes of the network, after a new check during each step.

Before permanently registering a transaction in the blockchain, the network performs several times a set of checks, including in particular that the outputs referenced by the inputs do exist and have not yet been used, that the author of the transaction is indeed the owner of the address credited in these outputs, and that the sum of the amounts appearing in the outputs of the transaction is much less than or equal to the sum of the amounts of the outputs referenced by the inputs. It is a bit complicated, but if you read this last sentence a couple of times you will get a better grasp of what actually happens during a transaction.

The effect of entering a transaction in the blockchain is to prohibit any future reference to the outputs designated by the inputs of this transaction, and therefore to prevent a double expenditure of the amount of these outputs, which would amount to creating from scratch bitcoins in an unauthorized manner. The only allowed creation of bitcoin from scratch is through a special transaction called Coinbase (not the exchange) inserted at the start of each block in the chain to pay the miner who inserted the block.

A transaction is taken into account instantly by the network and confirmed for the first time after approximately 10 minutes. Each new confirmation reinforces the validity of the transaction in the transaction register.

Bitcoin addresses

Each user can have any number of addresses that can be created through the wallet. Each bitcoin address has a public key and a private key pair associated with it.

An address is equal to the 160-bit (20 bytes) cryptographic hash of its public key. A bitcoin address also has a prefix identifying the version number (0 by default) and a four-byte checksum. In all, a bitcoin address occupies 25 bytes.

An address is represented in ASCII format thanks to a dedicated encoding of 58 alphanumeric characters: upper and lower case numbers and letters, with the exception of the letters and numbers l, I, 0 and O, which Nakamoto excluded due to their resemblance in some typefaces.

Here is, as an example, the very first bitcoin address that received bitcoins.

1A1zP1eP5QGefi2DMPTfTL5SLmv7DivfNa106.

To use the sum contained in an output of an existing transaction crediting a bitcoin address, the user must make use in the input of a transaction of the private key corresponding to the address by signing the transaction. The network checks the validity of this signature using the public key associated with the credited address, using asymmetric cryptography techniques. The operation is repeated for each entry of the transaction.

Wallets

Each user's wallet contains their personal data, including the address, public key and private key of each of their accounts. It can also contain user-specific information built from the blockchain. For example the list of available transaction outputs or account balances.

The wallet software provides the functions of creating accounts, consulting accounts, constructing and sending transactions. There is a choice of wallet software for all varieties of devices including smartphones. They differ in the extent of their ancillary functions and in their user interface.

The information contained in a user's wallet is critical and must be strictly protected against any intrusion. If the private key of an account is lost, the user can no longer access the transactions that fund this account, nor create new transactions from it. His bitcoins are permanently lost and will stay forever in the database without being able to change address. In 2013, a user lost 7,500 bitcoins, at the time worth $7.5 million, by accidentally throwing away the hard drive that contained his private key.

The discovery of the private key of an account by another user allows this one to steal the identity of the legitimate account holder and to spend the bitcoins which would come to be there, which is equivalent to the theft of bitcoins.

The mining process

The mining operation consists of assembling transactions into "blocks", by adding a header indicating in particular the size of the block, the number of transactions recorded, the date and time, a checksum ("hash") prohibiting any modification of the block and also serving as a unique identifier for the block, as well as the identifier of the previous block.

Miners include in the blocks they constitute a particular transaction which credits them with a certain number of bitcoins created for this purpose, and incorporates specific transaction fees. However, this remuneration will only be effective if the block is definitively accepted in the blockchain by the other nodes. It is this creation of money that explains the use of the term "mining", by analogy with the exploitation of gold mines.

A block can contain any number of transactions, typically between 1000 and 2000, but the block size cannot exceed 1 megabyte (for the Bitcoin Core system).

Within a block, transactions are stored in the form of a Merkle tree. The checksum (or fingerprint) of the block is calculated by applying twice a SHA-256 hash to the sextuplet made up of the following components.

- The software version number;
- the footprint of the header of the previous block;

- the root of the block's transaction tree (which is itself an indirect fingerprint of all the block's transactions);
- the timestamp (time elapsed since January 1, 1970, in seconds);
- the “nonce”.

The calculation of this footprint is made intentionally difficult by the requirement to be less than a certain value, which is materialized by a binary representation starting with a certain number of zeros. To this end, the fingerprint contains among its components, an arbitrary 32-bit number, called the “nonce”.

Even if one knows the hashes corresponding to certain nonces, the hashing makes it impossible to determine the value of the hash for a new nonce without running the algorithm again. Therefore, we can only find the appropriate nonce for the bound requirement on the value of the fingerprint by making several tests.

For a given value of the nonce, the probability of calculating a footprint less than the difficulty is very low, so many attempts must be made before this is achieved. Between 2014 and 2016, the average number of nonces that each miner had to test between each creation of blocks increased from 1 billion to 200 billion. This calculation consists of performing the same calculation a very large number of times from different data, so it lends itself well to parallel calculation.

The difficulty is readjusted every 2016 blocks to take into account the real computing power of the network and allows on average to add a block every 10 minutes, which amounts to saying that the probable duration of calculation of a valid footprint is 10 minutes for the most powerful computer or group of computers on the network.

This system of proof of work and chaining of blocks by their footprint makes any alteration of the blockchain practically impossible (except in the case of a 51% attack). An attacker who wishes to modify a transaction in a given block would be forced to recalculate his checksum and that of all subsequent blocks. As the difficulty increases over time, as does the number of blocks after the modified transaction (its degree of confirmation), the time required to make such a modification increases very rapidly.

When a miner has built a valid block whose checksum satisfies the difficulty condition, it broadcasts it to neighboring nodes, who check its validity before reposting it in turn. The remuneration for mining work is made in bitcoin. The payout is known as the block reward. The current block reward is 6.25 bitcoins. This reward is halved for every 210,000 blocks.

The valid blocks are thus broadcast step by step to all the nodes of the network, not without having been checked beforehand, but without being able to be modified. From the nonce included in the header, it is quick and easy to check the validity of the block (a simplistic parallel can be made with a sudoku game: its resolution is difficult and requires time and human calculation but its verification is very easy once the solution is found).

The environment dilemma

Mining is an activity often criticized because of the supposed environmental imprint of its energy consumption. However, some observers weigh down the criticism by pointing out that the "classic" monetary network consumes much more energy, through millions of cash dispensers or the infrastructures necessary for the proper functioning of the classic monetary system, such as data centers. The majority of bitcoin miners use renewable energy because it is cheaper in regions of the world that favor mining (low temperature, presence of dams, geothermal energy, etc.).

Estimate of power consumption

The power consumption of Bitcoin mining is difficult to assess due to the decentralization of the activity. The figures most often cited by the press come from the "Digiconomist" site created by a Dutch financial analyst.

According to his estimate, which is based on the assumption of an economic balance between mining revenues and costs, the global electricity consumption caused by mining would be 71.1 TWh / year (1 terawatt-hour (TWh) = 1 billion kilowatt-hours (kWh)). This would totat to about 0.32% of global electricity consumption.

With only around 200,000 transactions per day in 2018, Bitcoin's electricity consumption would be around 1,000 kWh per transaction on July 1st, 2018. By comparison Visa consumed 0.19 TWh / year to manage 111 billion dollars. transactions in 2017 (around 300 million transactions per day), i.e. 0.001 7 kWh per transaction. Bitcoin would thus consume approximately 600,000 times more energy per transaction than Visa. Note, however, that mining consumption is independent of the number of transactions.

The estimates of the “Digiconomist” site are nevertheless contested and considered exaggerated. In fact, according to Marc Bevand, a computer security engineer, they overestimate the power consumption of

Bitcoin miners by a factor of 1.5 to 2.8 (probably 2.2), which would reduce the total power consumption to 32.3 TWh / year, or 424 kWh per transaction (the equivalent of the consumption of a 1000 W radiator operating for almost 18 days).

These estimates are marred by uncertainties due to the assumptions they require, but it is possible to calculate a minimum power consumption of the Bitcoin network from verifiable data.

- The number of hashes per second: 37.1 × 1018 H / s on July 1st, 2018;
- the power and chopping capacity of the most efficient machine on the market (Bitmain's Antminer S9): 1323 W for 13.5 × 1012 H / s.

It is thus possible to affirm that the Bitcoin network had at least 2.8 million mining machines on July 1st, 2018 and that its electricity consumption was at least equal to 32.2 TWh / year. The number of entities securing the Bitcoin network is constantly increasing which increases the value of bitcoins.

According to a Bank of America report published in March 2021, the bitcoin network consumed 0.4% of global electricity at the end of 2020, or about as much as the Netherlands, and emits as many greenhouse gases as oil burned by American Airlines. In two years, these emissions have increased by 40 million tonnes, the equivalent of 8.3 million cars, to reach 60 million tonnes. Three quarters of the world's mining capacity is based in China; 27% of Chinese miners are in Sichuan, a province with strong low-carbon hydroelectric production, but 43% are in Xinjiang, where 80% of electricity comes from coal-fired power stations.

Why is power consumption so important?

The very high energy consumption of Bitcoin is linked to the new block mining system, which is supposed to protect the system from fraud in the absence of a central authority. Security is based on a mathematical problem the solution of which is difficult to find and the resolution of which is inherently expensive. To have a chance of adding the next block to the chain, miners must indeed invest heavily in server farms in order to have great computing power. These farms use a lot of electricity to power and cool the servers.

To be able to register a new block on the blockchain, miners must solve a mathematical problem submitted to everyone who competes, and it is the first who finds a solution that proceeds to the registration and earns a fee in bitcoins. Since the solution can only be found by trial and error, it is the miner who is able to make the maximum number of tries who has the most chance of winning. The difficulty of the problem is adjusted so that the computation time necessary for its resolution is of the order of 10 minutes.

The magnitude of the electricity consumption is linked to the intensity of the calculations and to the fact that these calculations are made simultaneously by a large number of miners. It is linked to the price of Bitcoin, because the higher it is, the more the remuneration increases and the more miners there are. This is reminiscent of Henry Ford's prediction at the start of the twentieth century: "An energy currency will replace gold and end wars".

According to Fabrice Flipo and Michel Berne, of the Institut Mines-Télécom, the generalization of crypto-currencies could lead to an energy consumption greater than eight times the electricity consumption of France, i.e. twice that of the United States, because their security and the confidence we have in them are based on a mathematical problem whose answer is difficult to find and whose resolution is in essence expensive.

The optimization of equipment and technical progress would make it possible to consume only 417 MW by 2021, which would nevertheless require nearly 5,500 kWh to produce a bitcoin, i.e. half of the annual electricity consumption of an American household.

Thus, for researcher Nicolas Houy, of the Lyon/Saint-Étienne Analysis and Economic Theory Group, “a large amount of money could very well be managed by a small amount of miners”.

Groups of miners

The difficulty of mining has led miners to group together in mining pools to combine their computing resources and build new blocks more quickly. The remuneration corresponding to the constitution of each block is then divided proportionally between the members, after deduction of fees, which makes it possible to smooth their income and makes them less uncertain. In 2016, around ten of these cooperatives supplied 95% of the blocks. They are largely found in China (which accounts for most of the hash energy on the bitcoin network), but also in the Czech Republic and Georgia.

Remuneration for mining activities has led to the development of ever more specialized technologies. The most efficient hardware uses integrated circuits that outperform general-purpose processors while using less power. As of 2015, a miner not using equipment specially designed for mining had a low probability of covering his electricity and equipment costs, even by joining a mining group.

Chapter 5

The Blockchain

The blockchain of the Bitcoin system is comparable to a public ledger recording transactions. It exists in more than 10,000 copies managed in parallel by the nodes of the network, none playing a privileged role. Some copies of the register are stored in areas safe from any cataclysm, such as in a bunker under the mountains in Switzerland.

The operator of each node in the network can decide to install a "full node" which builds and maintains a local copy of the blockchain. On the contrary, the operator can choose to be satisfied with a lightweight node which will call on the neighboring full nodes to validate the transactions using the SPV (simple payment verification) protocol.

Since these decisions are completely decentralized, it is impossible to know the number of nodes of each type. The only type permanently identified by specialized sites such as blockchain.info or bitnodes is that of "listening nodes" which accept, at the time of measurement, transactions and blocks from other nodes. Their number hovers around 10,000.

Network nodes are likely to number in the tens of thousands. For full nodes, the number of which matches the number of copies in the blockchain, estimates range from 5,000 to 30,000, located in 85 countries on all continents.

This redundancy ensures continuity of service. Each computer can become disconnected or crash without jeopardizing the proper functioning of the entire system. When it becomes operational again, the blockchain construction protocol it hosts automatically reconstructs the missing portion by resorting to neighboring nodes.
As long as they have access to the Internet, a user will always find a node in the network to accept and relay a

write-in, and then there will be a large number of miners and full nodes, located all over the world, to register that write-up and make it accessible in the blockchain, where it will always remain accessible from any point in the world with Internet access, without being able to be modified.

This same redundancy, together with the "precautionary principle" under which each node of the network checks the validity of the information it receives before using it, makes it impossible to propagate fraudulent activities. Errors and frauds are still possible on a particular computer, whether caused by the operator of the site or by a hacker who manipulates this site; it is even possible that they are spread locally by contagion or by connivance. On the other hand, it is virtually impossible for such issues to spread to a significant percentage of the copies of the blockchain, let alone the entire network.

The construction of the blockchain

By receiving a new block, each computer managing a complete node executes a protocol leading either to the rejection of the block if it has already been received or if it is invalid, or to its addition to the local blockchain after a final check of all the writings it contains, or when it is put on hold.

Each block contains the identifier of the block that precedes it in its miner's blockchain and, in the most common case, this predecessor is the terminal block of the local chain, to which the new block is added after a final verification of its validity. The transactions contained in this new block are then validated by the node, in particular the one which pays in bitcoins the miner who created this block. This is transmitted to neighboring nodes and, step by step, to the entire network. In the event of failure during the verification of the validity of the block, it is kept pending, and is incorporated into a secondary branch of the blockchain.

If the node receives a new block that contains a transaction already present in the local chain, that block is rejected. It is therefore the first valid block received that each node will register in its chain of blocks. Identical blocks built by other miners in the same 10 minute cycle will be rejected, so the miners race to see their blocks added to the chain and are paid accordingly.

Due to the delay required for the blocks to propagate through the network, two blocks created in the same cycle can arrive in a different order depending on the receiving nodes, which then build different versions of the register. In this case, we say that there is a fork. Most of the time, a fork is temporary, and the blockchain construction protocol corrects it in the next cycle.

The consensus mechanism

In order for all copies of the blockchain to be identical on all nodes, even though they are built independently, this protocol incorporates a so-called "consensus" mechanism, which is a central part of the system. The rule used by Bitcoin is to retain the chain whose construction of the blocks that make it up has required the most important work. To this end, the header of each block indicates the difficulty of the work that was done to build it. The fact that the checksum of the block respects the imposed constraints constitutes the “proof of work” guaranteeing that this work has been carried out.

If, after adding a block to a secondary chain, it appears that the secondary chain required more work than the main chain, that secondary chain should become the main branch. To do this, the program goes back to where it was detached from the main branch, revalidates the blocks and the transactions they contain one by one, and adds each block at the end of the new chain being processed.

This very complex process is the real heart of the system because it is the only way to change the blockchain and its results are irreversible. It also provides functions such as the resolution of bifurcation cases and the reconstruction of the chain in the event of a computer or network shutdown.

At the end of this second phase, each of the thousands of copies of the blockchain that exist on the complete nodes was extended by a block chosen by each node from among the proposals of the miners by applying the programmed consensus rule. If all full nodes implement the same write and block validation rules, this additional block is the same for all nodes, so that all copies of the blockchain remain the same. A few thousand new transactions are thus recorded definitively and become accessible on the thousands of corresponding sites.

The role of cryptography

Cryptography is used to authenticate actors, but digital data is not encrypted: cryptography is only used to ensure the signature.

Signature keys

To be valid, each transaction must be signed, in the cryptographic sense of the term, using asymmetric cryptography techniques. To this end, each bitcoin address also constitutes the cryptographic fingerprint of a public key. Any transaction indicates as input the reference of a previous transaction justifying the availability of funds subject to the transaction and as output one or more bitcoin addresses and the amounts that must be allocated to them. A transaction always balances its inputs and outputs.

To transmit bitcoins, a user must cryptographically sign a transaction referring as input to one or more previous transactions whose output amount is sufficient to cover the transaction. The private key used to sign this transaction must match the public key that previously received bitcoins. Therefore, the user must store all his private keys in a confidential and secure manner. The corresponding file in the software, called wallet.dat, must be kept and saved by the user in a confidential manner.

Cryptography enables the authentication and non-repudiation described above, through transaction signing and one-way functions. At no time does the system ensure the confidentiality or encryption of data transmitted over the network. All transactions are therefore in the clear.

The signing of transactions is performed using elliptical curve cryptography, known as ECDSA. In this case, the curve used is secp256k1.

Transparency

Even if the software does not use any personal data of the user, anonymity is not guaranteed. In fact, the identity of a user can be determined if the IP address is traceable, or possibly as a result of a meticulous and complex statistical study of the transaction database, or when the regulations of a state or group of states take legal steps to end the anonymity of transactions on virtual currency platforms. However, it is possible to remain anonymous on the Bitcoin network with so-called "mixing" services and a good knowledge of

AML, and KYC measures applied to exchange platforms.

The Bitcoin system does not encrypt any of the data it uses. Cryptography is only used to create tamper-proof signatures and implement one-way functions. Only the private key wallet is likely to be encrypted by the user, but this is optional.

Proof of work

Bitcoin uses the proof of work method, initially imagined to solve the spam problem and in particular implemented in the Hashcash system. The hash algorithms are SHA-256 and RIPEMD-160. A double hash in SHA-256 is used to obtain the hash of the blocks and therefore the proof of work, while a SHA-256 followed by a RIPEMD-160 is used to construct the bitcoin addresses.

Chapter 6

The specific features of Bitcoin

The Bitcoin system's unit of account is bitcoin. The symbols used to represent it are BTC and XBT. Bitcoin can also be subdivided into smaller units such as millibitcoin (mXBT), microbitcoin (μXBT) or even satoshi, which represents 10 nano bitcoins (10nXBT). Microbitcoin is sometimes referred to as a bit.

The Unicode consortium agreed in November 2015 to add bitcoin among its characters, assigning it the code 20BF.

Specificities of Bitcoin

As a virtual currency, bitcoin has three particularities.

- In terms of regulation, the lack of legal status and regulatory framework means that virtual currencies do not provide any guarantee of price or liquidity. The voluntary limitation of the number of units issued without indexation carries a risk of speculation leading to high volatility.

- In terms of transparency, encryption of the identities of beneficiaries and order givers leads to total anonymity of transactions. The transactions carried out are recorded in a public register, but this traceability is limited. In fact, it does not allow to know the principal and the beneficial owner, it is neither certain nor systematic, it cannot be exploited neither technically nor legally.

- In terms of extraterritoriality, the protagonists, the servers and the legal persons who exploit them may be located in countries and territories whose cooperation may be difficult to obtain.

Exchange terminals allow bitcoin virtual currency to be exchanged for legal tender, much like an ATM can withdraw cash from a bank. To do this, these terminals can take into account identification formalities based on biometric control: taking palm prints, scanning an identity document and comparing facial features with the photo that appears on the identity card.

Another particularity of Bitcoin is the irrevocability of an illicit transaction, which makes it extremely important to be sure to send the funds to a correct address.

Proof of ownership

The user who owns bitcoins can access them through a specific address and a password also known as a private key. Since knowledge of the private key is essential for signing transactions, bitcoins cannot be spent without resorting to it. The network checks the validity of the private key using the user's public key with asymmetric cryptography techniques. On the other hand, only knowledge of the public key of an address is necessary to make a deposit. You can imagine the public key to be your bank account number, while the private key is the password to access your home banking.

Transactions and fees

Bitcoins from different transactions cannot be combined. A user receiving several payments will keep as many different amounts (called input data) in their wallet, even if their software, to make them easier to read, displays the total amount. When the user wants to spend them, their software will calculate the best set of input data to transfer to minimize the size of the output data and thus limit transaction costs.

Example: a user receives 13 payments of 1 × 2.3 XBT, 5 × 1.0 XBT, 2 × 0.7 XBT, 1 × 0.5 XBT, 1 × 0.3 XBT, 2 ×

0.2 XBT and 1 × 0.1 XBT. The software will tell them that they have 10.0 XBT.
(Case 1): If they want to spend 3.0 XBT, the best set of output data will be to combine the 2.3 XBT and 0.7 XBT received previously.
(Case 2): If they want to spend 3.05 XBT, the best output data set is to bundle the 2.3 XBT with the 0.7 XBT received previously and split the transaction from 0.1 XBT into one exit transaction of 0.05 XBT, the other transaction fraction of 0.05 XBT being kept in the wallet.

As you can see, this process is quite complicated and requires a few internal transactions. The beauty of the Bitcoin network is that the end user does not need to do anything. Once the transaction has been issued, everything is done automatically.

The payment of transaction fees is theoretically optional, but the miners determine the order of processing of the transactions to be integrated into the new blocks according to the transaction fees offered by the users. The more a user accepts to pay high transaction fees, the faster their transaction will be processed. In the event of charges of the same amount, priority is given to the oldest transactions. Transactions made without transaction fees are processed after all others; in practice, these transactions start to be processed on average from 120 minutes and up to a potentially infinite time.

The most competitive transaction fees, which provide almost immediate confirmation, between 0 and 35 minutes on average, are around 80 satoshis / byte (0,000,000 80 XBT / byte). Thus, in 2016, for a median transaction size of 265 bytes, this represents an approximate cost of 21,200 satoshis (or less than $0.11) regardless of the amount of bitcoins to be transferred.

To discourage the proliferation of low-value transactions, the software applies a mandatory transaction fee of 0.0001 XBT to any transaction for an amount less than 0.01 XBT.

The larger the assemblies of input data are to carry out a transaction, the longer it takes to encode and the more the costs increase, while still remaining a very low overall amount. The algorithm of the Bitcoin software is designed to avoid as much as possible the aggregation of input data of amount less than 0.01 XBT in order to limit mandatory transaction fees.

If the amount of bitcoins to be transferred is low or if the transaction is recent, only the payment of transaction fees will allow immediate processing of the transaction. In fact, each transaction is assigned an order of priority determined as a function of its amount, its age and its size, itself determined as a function of the number of input data grouped together. Specifically, the software calculates a quotient determined by the number of bitcoins to be transferred multiplied by the age of the transaction and divided by the size of the aggregated input data. Below a certain quotient, the transaction will only be processed immediately in return for the payment of transaction fees.

If the user chooses not to pay transaction fees, the quotient will increase over time until it exceeds a threshold value which will trigger the processing of the transaction; it will thus be processed free of charge but with delay.

The higher the number of bitcoins to be transferred, the higher the quotient and the faster the user will see their transaction processed or free of charge.
For the same amount of bitcoins to be transferred, transactions involving a small number of input data are processed faster than others. Bitcoin software generally calculates the optimal fees to pay for the transaction to be processed at the time of transfer. These fees vary depending on the number of transactions to be processed at the time of the transfer, but overall they are very negligible. The user decides on their own how much transaction fees they are willing to pay.

Special cases

If a user has registered in their wallet 3 XBTs from two transactions of 1 and 2 XBT and wishes to purchase a product or service costing 2,999 XBT free of charge, the Bitcoin software will have to combine the two transactions and split the transaction of 1 XBT into one line of 0.999 XBT and one of 0.001 XBT. But in this case, the 0.001 XBT line would have an automatic charge of 0.0001 XBT applied. The user could not then make their purchase which would cost them 2 XBT + 0.999 XBT + 0.0001 XBT when they have 3 XBT and wish to keep 0.001 XBT. In such a case, it would be better for them to send 3 XBT to the seller free of charge, although some sellers want the exact purchase amount sent to them.

The reddit site reports the case of a user who won a jackpot of XBT 1,280 on a gambling site where the amount of bets was XBT 0.02. To transfer the jackpot amount, the gaming site had to aggregate 64,000 transactions amounting to XBT 0.02 in input data, which represented a 51,203 byte transaction; the amount of fees required for immediate processing was 0.026 XBT, or approximately $15, which is more than the player's bet amount, $12, or than a fee usually paid for a normal transaction- Some miners may choose to process transactions by breaking the rules of the Bitcoin protocol. In this case, they include the transaction in a new block that they will manage to mine in a longer time as their computing power is low.

The creation of bitcoins

The creation of a new block is rewarded with bitcoins created for this purpose. The amount of this reward is halved every time 210,000 transaction blocks are added to the blockchain. This process is called the "halving" and it is one of the fundamental reasons that sustain the price increase of bitcoin. Here is how it works.

From the creation of the first block (genesis block) to the 209,999th block, created on November 28, 2012, each miner was rewarded with 50 newly created bitcoins for the creation of a new valid block. From block 210,000 to block 419,999, created on July 9th, 2016, the reward was 25 bitcoins for each newly created block. From block 420,000 to block 629,999, created on May 11th, 2020, the reward was 12.5 bitcoins for each newly created block. From block

630,000 to block 839,999, the reward is 6.25 bitcoins for each newly created block.

The next halving should take place around May 2024, when the reward will decrease to 3.125 bitcoins per block.

The reward system tends towards zero as the series of 210,000 blocks follow one another, so that a maximum of 20,999,999.9769 bitcoins will be created, probably around the year 2140. The gradual decrease in the amount of new bitcoins rewarding the creation of new blocks will be offset by the development of transaction fees.

In other words, the inventor of the Bitcoin system tried to define a monetary policy whereby the number of bitcoins cannot exceed 21 million units in total, with the rate of creation of new units tending towards zero. Such a monetary system is described as deflationary. As you might know, the Dollar-based system is inflationary, as more units are printed to sustain the growth of the economy.

Confidentiality

The Bitcoin system indicates on the public ledger the amount of bitcoins associated with each address. All transactions recorded on the blockchain are also public. The identity of the owners of bitcoin addresses is not public but can be determined, for example through exchange platforms that record the identity of their users.

Exchange platforms generally pool their users' holdings on a single address and reallocate a bitcoin credit line to each of their users through their trading software. Users can thus exchange their bitcoins for other cryptocurrencies or for currencies. The platform secures its deposits by distributing them over several addresses or by storing them to prevent any theft. When a user transfers the deposits from the platform to another address, the platform debits the credit line and transfers the amount to be exchanged from one of his addresses to the address indicated by the user.

Researchers at Stanford University and Concordia University have shown that, to prevent hacking, bitcoin exchange platforms can prove their creditworthiness without revealing their addresses using zero-knowledge protocols.

It is also possible to keep bitcoins in "cold storage" on a digital medium disconnected from the network, which has the effect of protecting them against theft. Between 2017 and 2018, a French start-up sold more than 1.5 million of these bitcoin safes in 165 countries Nowadays, Ledger and Trezor are the two main companies that sell hard wallets.

Researchers have argued that in the absence of specific protection measures, payments made using the Bitcoin protocol are no more private than payments by bank card.

Stock exchanges and financial instruments

Bitcoin, as a virtual currency, is quite unclassifiable. Thus, some asset management companies consider that virtual currency can neither be considered as a good investment, nor be compared to gold, due to the lack of price history.

For the ex-president of the SEC, Jay Clayton, the "Initial Coin Offerings" are less protected than the traditional securities, allowing more manipulation of markets and scams. For him, as for other investments, extreme caution as well as awareness of the risk of losing everything is required.

No ICOs have been registered with the US federal financial markets regulator and supervisor (known as the SEC), and the listing and trading of exchange traded products that hold cryptocurrency has not been approved by the SEC up to this point.

Market platforms

Fiduciary currencies (USD, EUR, CNY, etc.) or crypto-currencies (ETH, LTC, etc.) can be exchanged for bitcoins through various exchanges or specialized trading platforms active on the internet, by carrying out transactions transfers by bank transfer. Brokerage fees are generally very low and users must provide proof of their identity to access these platforms. As you might think, in this way the anonymity of Bitcoin disappears.

Escrow platforms connect buyers and sellers to exchange bitcoins for cash, money orders, or bank transfers.
One-way points of sale make it possible to pay in bitcoins, subject to the payment of a fee, by debiting the corresponding amount in dollars on bank cards or prepaid cards.

Finally, there are vending machines which charge a generally higher commission.

Since November 2016, the Swiss Federal Railways have been offering, in conjunction with the company SweePay, the purchase of bitcoins from their train ticket machines, thus creating the largest bitcoin distribution network in the world.

Chapter 7

Satoshi Nakamoto

As we have seen, the creation of the Bitcoin network is still a mystery. In this chapter we try to gather all the information there is regarding the identity of Satoshi Nakamoto. Please, keep in mind that his identity has never been revealed and that we can only make assumptions on who he actually is.

Satoshi Nakamoto is the pseudonym of the inventor of the cryptocurrency Bitcoin.

In November 2008, Satoshi Nakamoto published the Bitcoin protocol on The Cryptography Mailing list on the metzdowd.com website. In 2009 he distributed the first version of the client software and later contributed to the project anonymously together with other developers, to finally withdraw from the Bitcoin community in 2010. The last contact from Satoshi Nakamoto was in 2011, when he claimed to have moved on to other projects and left Bitcoin in good hands with Gavin Andresen.

The theories about Satoshi Nakamoto's true identity are numerous. Nobody knows if it is a "he", a "she" or if it is more than one person. In Japanese "satoshi" means "clear, quick and wise thought". "Naka" can mean "medium", "inside" or "relationship". "Moto" can mean "origin" or "foundation". But it is not certain whether these meanings are useful to trace back to the person or group of people who invented the Bitcoin system.

It was originally thought to be Michael Clear, a graduate in cryptography from Trinity College but he denied. Others suspected Vili Lehdonvirta, a former Finnish game developer (but also a sociologist and economist), but he too has denied any connection with Satoshi.

Adam Penenberg, a professor at New York University, claims that behind the mysterious character there are three people: Neal King, Vladimir Oksman, Charles Bry. Penenberg's thesis is based on a Google search of some particular phrases of the bitcoin protocol that lead back to a patent request for updating and distributing cryptographic keys. The patent was applied for by King, Oksman and Bry, who denied having anything to do with bitcoin.

Nick Szabo, a computer scientist and cryptographer, has long been suspected of being Satoshi along with collaborator Laszlo Hanyecz. Both have always firmly denied, but in the next pages we are going to tell you more about Szabo, as he is the one we believe to be Satoshi.

Others think it is Martii Malmi, a Finnish developer, who dealt with Bitcoin from the very beginning by also creating the user interface of the system. There are also rumors about the creator of MtGox, Jed McCaleb, an American lover of Japanese culture and resident in Japan. Other theories instead lead to Donal O'Mahony and Michael Peirce, who wrote a paper on digital payments in e-commerce platforms.

In 2017, after a tip from a SpaceX employee, the idea appeared on the web that Elon Musk was hiding behind the pseudonym, a theory later denied by the entrepreneur himself on his Twitter account.

Craig Steven Wright

In December 2015, according to two investigative articles published by Wired and Gizmodo, Craig Steven Wright, an Australian entrepreneur, would be the creator of Bitcoin. Within hours, searches were carried out in Wright's home and office by the Australian Federal Police, however unrelated to the incident.

On May 2nd, 2016, Craig Steven Wright publicly claimed to be Satoshi Nakamoto. Wright revealed his identity to the BBC, The Economist and GQ. In order to prove his claim, he signed a message with the private encryption key associated with the first Bitcoin transaction. However, the validation of this signature is disputed and even if its validity were demonstrated, many cryptographic experts do not consider it a definitive proof, as it refers to the second block and not to the first created.

On May 4th, 2016, Wright promised to publish further evidence to prove his identity. However, the next day, he deleted all posts on his blog and published a note titled "I'm sorry" in which he declared that he was ready to publish more evidence but did not have the courage to do so. He ended the note with a "goodbye". In the same year Wright filed a copyright request for the Bitcoin white paper, originally written by Satoshi Nakamoto. However, the copyright request was denied due to insufficient proof of ownership.

Nick Szabo

We admit it: our opinion is that Nick Szabo is Satoshi Nakamoto. We have no actual proof of his identity, but after having researched this subject quite extensively this is our opinion.

Nick Szabo is a computer scientist, lawyer, and cryptographer known for his research on digital contracts and digital currency. He graduated from the University of Washington in 1989 with a degree in computer science.The expression and concept of "smart contracts" were developed by Szabo with the aim of bringing what he calls "highly evolved" practices of contract law, from the conception to the application of the protocols of contract between strangers on the Internet. Smart contracts are a major feature of cryptocurrencies and the programming language E.

Szabo worked for David Chaum, the inventor of electronic money "E-Cash" as a consultant in the mid-90s. In 1998, Szabo designed a decentralized digital currency mechanism which he called "Bit gold". Bit gold, not having received enough support, was never implemented, but was referred to as a direct precursor to the Bitcoin architecture.

In the principle of Bit gold, participants devote the power of their computers to solving cryptographic puzzles. The solved puzzles are sent to a public registry insensitive to the problem of the Byzantine generals, and assigned to the public key of the participant who solved the puzzle. Each solution is then integrated into the input data of the next challenge, creating an increasingly long chain. Until the majority of participants agree to a solution for the current riddle, the work of solving the next riddle cannot begin. It is a proof-of-work-type consensus model. This also makes it possible to manage the issuance of new Bit gold tokens as well as a means of checking their timestamp.

The main problem with transactions in digital form is the so-called double-spending problem. Once the data has been created, reproducing it is a simple matter of copying and pasting. Most digital currencies solve the problem by ceding some control to a central authority that keeps track of the balance of each account. This was considered unacceptable by Szabo. In an interview he stated the following. "I sought to imitate as closely as possible in cyberspace the security and trust characteristics of gold, and the main one is that it does not depend on any central authority".

In 2008, a mysterious figure writing under the pseudonym Satoshi Nakamoto published a proposal for Bitcoin. As you know Nakamoto's true identity has since remained a secret, leading to speculation about a long list of people suspected of being Nakamoto. Although Szabo has repeatedly denied it, some people (including us) have speculated that he was Nakamoto.

Research by financial author Dominic Frisby provides circumstantial evidence of this, but, as he admits, no formal evidence that Satoshi is indeed Szabo. In a July 2014 email from Frisby, Szabo said, "Thanks for letting me know this. I'm afraid you are wrong in exposing me as Satoshi, but I'm used to this".

Nathaniel Popper wrote in the New York Times that the most convincing evidence regarding the creation of

Bitcoin pointed to an American man of Hungarian descent by the name of Nick Szabo. In 2008, prior to the publication of Bitcoin, Szabo wrote a comment on his blog about the intention to create a working version of his hypothetical currency. This blog post is exactly what makes us think he is the actual inventor of this amazing monetary network.

Chapter 8

The Byzantine Generals Problem

In the previous chapters, we have mentioned the Byzantine generals problem a few times. In the next few pages we are going to dive deeper into this subject and understand why Bitcoin offers an amazing solution to this issue.

The problem of the Byzantine generals is a computer problem on how to reach consensus in situations where errors are possible. In particular, in distributed computer systems there may be imperfect information for the failure of a component, such as a server, and it can appear inconsistent, non-functional and functioning for fault detection systems, presenting different symptoms to different observers.

The problem

The problem of the Byzantine generals refers to a problem of agreement (described by Leslie Lamport, Robert Shostak and Marshall Pease in their 1982 article "The problem of the Byzantine generals") in which a group of generals commands part of the Byzantine army. Surrounded by a city, these generals want to formulate a plan to attack it. In its simplest form, generals should only decide whether to attack or retreat, and some generals prefer to attack, while others prefer to retreat. The important thing is that each general accepts a common decision, as a solitary attack by some generals would result in a defeat and would be worse than a coordinated attack or a coordinated withdrawal.

The problem is complicated by the presence of traitorous generals who not only vote for a suboptimal strategy, but can do so selectively. For example, if nine generals vote, four of whom support the attack while the other four are in favor of the withdrawal, the ninth general can send a vote of withdrawal to those generals in favor of the withdrawal and an attack vote to the others. Those who have received a vote of withdrawal from the ninth general will withdraw, while the rest will attack. The problem is further complicated by the fact that the generals are physically separated and must send their votes through messengers who may not report the votes or falsify them.

Byzantine fault tolerance can be achieved if loyal (non-defective) generals find majority agreement on their strategy. Note that there may be a default vote value for lost messages. For example, missing messages can be assigned the value <null>. In addition, if the agreement provides that the <null> votes are the majority, it is possible to use a pre-established strategy (for example, withdrawal).

The typical mapping of this story into computer systems is that computers are the generals and their connections to the digital communications system are the messengers. Although the problem is formulated in the analogy as a decision-making and security problem, in electronics it cannot be solved simply with cryptographic digital signatures, since errors such as incorrect voltages can be propagated through the encryption process. Therefore, a component may appear to be functional for one component and defective for another component, which prevents a consensus on whether the component is defective or not.

Examples of Byzantine errors

In a similar problem, bee swarms are used as an example. They have to find a new home, and the bees have to reach a consensus on which of the candidate homes they can reach. And then everyone has to fly there, with their queen. The bee approach works reliably, but when researchers find two houses, equally attractive by all bee criteria, a catastrophe occurs, the swarm breaks up and all the bees die.

First solutions

In 1982 Lamport, Shostak and Pease described several solutions. They began by pointing out that the problem of generals can be reduced to solve a "commander and lieutenant" problem in which loyal lieutenants must act in group and that their action must correspond to that the commander has ordered in case the commander is loyal.

One solution considers scenarios in which messages can be falsified, but which will be tolerant of Byzantine flaws as long as the number of traitorous generals does not equal or exceed one third of the generals. The inability to deal with a third or more of the traitors ultimately boils down to proving that the problem of one commander and two lieutenants cannot be solved if the commander is a traitor. To see this, suppose we have a treacherous commander A and two lieutenants, B and C. When A tells B to attack and C to retreat, and B and C exchange messages, relaying the message from A, neither B nor C can find out who the traitor is, since it is not necessarily A. In fact, another lieutenant could have falsified the message presumably from A.

It can be shown that if “n” is the number of generals in total, and “t” is the number of traitors in that n, there are solutions to the problem only when n>3t and the communication is synchronous.

A second solution requires unforced message signatures. For critical security systems, digital signatures (in modern computer systems, this can be achieved in practice using public key cryptography) can provide tolerance to Byzantine flaws in the presence of an arbitrary number of traitorous generals.

There is also a variation of the first two solutions that allow for behavior tolerant to Byzantine errors in some situations where not all generals can communicate directly with each other.

Around 1980, several system architectures that implemented Byzantine fault tolerance were designed. These include: Draper's FTMP, Honeywell13's 12 MMFC, and SRI.14's SIFT

Fault tolerance

In 1999, Miguel Castro and Barbara Liskov introduced the "BFT (Byzantine Fault Tolerance) algorithm. In a nutshell, Byzantine fault tolerance (BFT) is the property of a system that can resist the class of failures derived from the Byzantine generals Problem. This means that a BFT system is able to continue operating even if some nodes fail or act dishonestly.

There is more than one solution to the Byzantine generals problem and, consequently, more than one way to build a BFT system. Likewise, there are various different approaches for a blockchain that intends to achieve Byzantine fault tolerance. This brings us to so-called consensus algorithms.

Bitcoin and the BFT algorithm

An example of BFT in use is bitcoin, a peer-to-peer digital currency system. The bitcoin network works in parallel to generate a Hashcash-style work test chain. The proof-of-work chain is the key to overcoming

Byzantine failures and obtaining a coherent global view of the state of the system.

We can define a consensus algorithm as the mechanism by which a blockchain network achieves consensus. The most common implementations are proof of work (PoW) and proof of stake (PoS). Let's take the case of Bitcoin as an example.

While the Bitcoin protocol establishes the primary rules of the system, the PoW consensus algorithm is what defines the way these rules are followed to reach consensus (for example, when verifying and validating transactions). Even though the concept of proof of work is older than cryptocurrencies, Satoshi Nakamoto developed a modified version by creating an algorithm that allowed the creation of Bitcoin as a BFT system.

It should be remembered that the PoW algorithm is not 100% Byzantine fault tolerant, but thanks to the expensive mining process and the underlying cryptographic techniques, PoW has proved to be one of the safest and most reliable implementations for blockchain networks. In this sense, the Proof of Work consensus algorithm, designed by Satoshi Nakamoto, is considered by many to be one of the most ingenious solutions to the Byzantine Generals Problem.

As we have seen, the Byzantine Generals Problem is an interesting dilemma that eventually gave rise to BFT systems, which are widely applied in different scenarios. In addition to the blockchain sector, some use cases for BFT systems include aviation, space industry and nuclear energy.

In the context of cryptocurrencies, having efficient network communication along with a valid consensus mechanism is vital for any blockchain ecosystem. Securing these systems is a constant effort, and existing consensus algorithms have not yet managed to overcome certain limitations (such as scalability). Despite this, PoW and PoS are very interesting approaches as BFT systems, and the potential applications are certainly inspiring widespread innovation.

Chapter 9

Legal framework

The legal nature of bitcoin is not a uniformly decided issue. The international aspect of bitcoin, with regard to the regional nature of the legal frameworks (European Union, United States, China, in particular), precludes any comprehensive legal response, in the current state of the law.

In particular, the G20 considered that if crypto assets raise issues with regards to consumer and investor protection, market integrity, tax evasion, money laundering and terrorist financing, then they must be managed by states rather than by the G20 itself.

European Union

According to the European Central Bank, the important banking and financial regulations imposed on the Member States of the European Union do not concern bitcoin. The European banking authority warned consumers against the risks associated with bitcoin (December 13th, 2013), considering cryptocurrencies as "virtual representations" of money. It also recommended on July 4th, 2014 to European banking and financial institutions not to use bitcoin nor to offer services around it.

On October 22nd, 2015, the Court of Justice of the European Union confirmed that bitcoin exchange transactions for traditional currencies were exempt from VAT, considering bitcoin as a "virtual currency" and not as a good or a service.

Australia

In December 2013, the Governor of the Central Bank of Australia (RBA) said in an interview on the legality of bitcoin that "there would be nothing to stop people from deciding to transact in another currency in a store if they wanted. There is no law against this, so we have competing currencies".

Australia has officially confirmed that bitcoin will be treated as cash on July 1st, 2017 and that it will no longer be subject to double taxation.

Belgium

The Minister of Finance indicated that government intervention with regard to the Bitcoin system does not appear to be necessary, since it is the European Union that should be focused on regulating this subject.

The central bank of Belgium estimated in a statement that "the threats to monetary stability posed by digital currencies issued by private actors are currently rather limited, because they used as a medium of exchange, so that their impact on the conditions in the economy is weak".

China

On December 5th, 2013, the Chinese Central Bank banned local banks from any bitcoin transaction, a measure leading to the start of a crash in the value of the virtual currency. BTC China, the world's leading bitcoin transaction platform, prohibited users from making new deposits in Yuan into their account "following new government regulations". On January 8th, 2014, the Chinese group Ali Baba banned bitcoin payments, in accordance with new Chinese regulations. A law established on September 4th, 2017 leads either to the closure of an exchange platform or to the end of the acceptance of fiat currencies. In February 2018, the Chinese government announced that it wanted to strengthen the ban through censorship of all Chinese or foreign bitcoin exchange websites.

South Korea

In South Korea bitcoin and cryptocurrencies are legal and recognized as financial instruments.

There are no restrictions for holding and exchanging bitcoin between individuals. Exchange platforms must ensure they have at least 500 million Korean Won to protect traders and businesses from embezzlement and fraud.

The government of South Korea has agreements with 14 "virtual cash" exchange platforms known as currency exchanges. Thanks to these agreements, these platforms only accept users whose identity is controlled by a financial actor such as a bank.

United States

The parliamentary report by Senator Tom Carper (February 3rd, 2014) provided a first overview of the legal issues of bitcoin.

The report concluded on the economic interest of bitcoin and the need to regulate its development, in order to contain its specific risks. It also did not offer a firm legal definition of bitcoin.

On February 26th, 2014, US Senator Joe Manchin called for bitcoin to be banned in the United States, because of its uncontrolled volatility and the risk that it could be used for illegal purposes, in particular for money laundering. For the moment, the United States considered that virtual currencies developed on the bitcoin model have no legal value but constitute assets liable to be subject to taxes.

On December 10th, 2017, the Chicago Stock Exchange institutionalized Bitcoin, launching the possibility to trade Bitcoin futures.

In 2018, the authorities - notably the Securities and Exchange Commission, and the Commodity Futures Trading Commission - prosecuted various actors who carried out scams such as the dangling of the possibility of getting rich with Bitcoin or binary options.

France

In France, neither the law nor case law has specifically and clearly regulated the nature and legal regime of bitcoin. For some lawyers, it is not a currency. For others, bitcoin would be "a currency, electronic in nature, devoid of legal tender". For the national commission of campaign accounts and political financing, it is a “currency without defined legal status”. For the Directorate General of Public Finances, bitcoin is considered to be a movable property, the value at purchase or sale and its value at the end of the fiscal year being legal.

In the event that Bitcoin is considered to be electronic money, the rules in force for electronic money would apply to bitcoin (Articles L. 133-29 et seq. 191 of the Monetary and Financial Code). In other cases, a legal regime for Bitcoin would have to be invented.

In a 2014 report it was stated that virtual currency did not represent a claim on the issuer and was not issued against the remittance of funds, within the meaning of the electronic money directive, which did not give it the electronic money status. On the other hand, no text excludes bitcoin transactions from the tax obligations in force, in particular with regard to the taxation of profits or the collection of capital gain tax. This situation was recalled by the tax authorities on July 11th, 2014. Similarly, profits made in accordance with the definition of article 92 of the General Tax Code (CGI) are subject to taxation.

In January 2018, the Minister of the Economy, Bruno Le Maire, said he understood “the risks of speculation and possible embezzlement”. He entrusted a mission on bitcoin to Jean-Pierre Landau, former deputy governor of the Banque de France. In his report, Jean-Pierre Landau recommends not directly regulating crypto-currencies (except in the context of the fight against money laundering), to create an environment favorable to the development of this technology and to strictly limit the exposure of the financial sector to cryptocurrencies. On September 12th, 2018, France became the first country in the world to grant a legal framework to Initial Coin Offerings.

Japan

The central bank of Japan officially recognizes bitcoin and cryptocurrencies as a means of payment. In fact, article 2-5 of the amended PSA specifies that virtual currencies are accepted as a means of payment without being legal currencies.

United Kingdom

Bitcoin is considered "private money". When cryptocurrencies are exchanged for pounds sterling or other fiat currencies, such as the euro or the dollar, no VAT is due. However, VAT applies for all goods and services that could be exchanged for bitcoins. Profits and losses made on cryptocurrencies are subject to capital gains tax.

Russia

On February 6th, 2014, Russia declared the currency illegal on its territory, arguing that the only official currency in Russia is the ruble and that no other currency can legally be used in the country.

Singapore

In December 2013, the Singapore Monetary Authority asserted that trading in goods and services for bitcoins constituted trade in which it was not for the authority to intervene.

In January 2014, Singapore's Domestic Revenue Administration released a set of tax guidelines according to which bitcoin transactions can be considered barter if they are used as a method of payment for real goods and services. Companies that deal in bitcoin exchanges will be taxed based on their sales levels.

Swiss

In Switzerland, the Federal Council considered that bitcoin is a virtual currency of marginal use, and that as such it is subject in principle to the legislation of regular currencies. However, it recommends that authorities and responsible consumer organizations call on bitcoin users to be cautious.

According to the Federal Council, the execution of contracts concluded in virtual currencies can in principle be ensured and offenses committed with these currencies are punishable.

For example, the professional trading of virtual currencies and the operation of trading platforms in Switzerland fall in principle within the scope of the law on money laundering, which requires the identity of the person to be verified.

However, from the Swiss point of view, there are no international standards regulating virtual currencies.

Bitcoin will always exist, whether prohibited or advised by the authorities, you just need to connect to the internet by cable or satellite to make a transaction in your ledger. In addition, people residing in countries hostile to bitcoin can use a method such as those proposed by Samourai or Wasabi, for example, to avoid being traced.

The debate around Bitcoin and terrorism

Various opinions relating to the real or supposed link between Bitcoin and terrorism have been raised.

On several occasions, Bitcoin has been touted as a tool that can be used for terrorist financing their criminal actions. In our opinion, stating that Bitcoin can be used for terrorism is as saying that dollars can be used for the same reason. Both statements could be true, but we will never consider stopping using dollars because of this potential issue.

Chapter 10

Potential Risks Linked to the Bitcoin Network

From the outset, Bitcoin has been the subject of many discussions, both technical and economic, and even political.

From these discussions, a number of advantages and disadvantages of the Bitcoin network were discussed. Some of these comments are not necessarily specific to bitcoin and could be applied to other payment systems with similar characteristics.

However, recently, we realized that the risks associated with bitcoin are little or poorly understood in their nature and extent.

Bitcoin, like most existing cryptocurrencies, has no underlying assets or collateral. Whoever buys a bitcoin exclusively pays the seller. Therefore, the increase in the value of money comes exclusively from the continued presence of a flow of buyers able to support its price. Therefore, on closer inspection, the functioning of bitcoin might seem much more similar to that of a pyramid system than to that of a monetary system. However, if you have followed us so far, you know that in reality things are quite different. In fact, when you store bitcoins you contribute to the stability and strength of the monetary network, which grows and strengthens itself from the amount of money that investors pour into it.

Volatility

Bitcoin is a volatile currency because the number of coins is limited in the face of growing demand. The price evolves according to the news on crypto-currencies. Cryptocurrency is floating like any currency and fluctuates differently against different currencies.

Irreversibility

A bitcoin transaction is irreversible and cannot be reversed. This means that if you give or type the wrong address, you will have lost your coins for good.

Depending on the internet

The Bitcoin protocol is an overlay of the IP protocol which is the basis of the functioning of the internet. In the event of an internet shutdown (massive power / IT failure or forced shutdown by a government of internet providers' routers, for example) or if a government does not promote or defend internet neutrality, the Bitcoin protocol could be slowed down or even completely blocked.

Technical limitations of the network

The size of the database has grown very rapidly and requires several gigabytes of memory in a hard drive. Some experts have questioned the future size of this database and are discussing possible solutions to save disk space such as pruning the oldest transactions that form the Merkle tree. However, this does not seem necessary given the progress made in storage technologies.

The size of the block is another important aspect. Bitcoin "super-nodes" are being considered to facilitate the propagation of information through the nodes of the network and which struggle to keep up with the increase in the size of the database. Some scholars argue that Moore's Law could help track network growth using personal computers.

Institutional risk

To convert cryptocurrency to currency it is often necessary to go through an exchange platform operated by private companies, which are potentially vulnerable to defaults or bankruptcies, as happened to Mt. Gox. However, it is possible to exchange your bitcoins for cash, gold or a service in order to avoid this pitfall.

Environmental impacts and risks

They are linked to the electricity consumption generated by mining, which represents, according to estimates, from 0.15% to 0.32% of the world electricity consumption. They are low when it is produced from renewable energies, but important for fossil fuels (global warming and air pollution). More and more server farms are installed in countries with cold climates (to facilitate their cooling) with cheap renewable energies, such as Canada and Iceland.

A study on the origin of the electricity consumed by mining farms shows that 74.1% of the energy consumed is produced from renewable energies. However, following criticism, the lead author of the study admitted there were some mistakes in the research. Indeed, the major renewable energy in China, hydroelectricity, is only available at low cost in certain periods of the year. The rest of the year electricity production comes mainly from coal.

Ethical risks

Bitcoin would favor the first acquirers of the currency ("early adopters"). This claim is sometimes confirmed by certain studies showing that the distribution of wealth in bitcoin is very unequal.

It has been suggested that Bitcoin could be likened to a Ponzi scheme, but this is not applicable as we have seen in the previous pages as well. In fact, the price of the cryptocurrency is a balance between buyers looking to acquire the currency and sellers looking to sell it. In a Ponzi scheme, new entrants pay early adopters and receive nothing in return.

Some central banks (ECB, Banque de France, Bank of China) have issued warnings on the use of bitcoin insisting on its highly speculative character, on the legal risks it generates due to its status as an unregulated currency and on its possible use for criminal purposes (money laundering, terrorist financing). The European Banking Authority (EBA) also issued a warning in December 2013 against the lack of consumer protection through the use of the payment method that is bitcoin. However, other institutions hold a more nuanced or even opposite approach. Thus, the German and American governments regard this currency with a certain benevolence and Ben Bernanke, ex-president of the FED, stated that bitcoin has potential to revolutionize the monetary system.

Chapter 11

Mixed Opinions on Bitcoin

Economists have expressed various opinions on bitcoin. For the American Nobel Laureate in Economics Joseph Stiglitz, bitcoin is a bubble that will be very exciting as long as it goes up before it goes down. For him, it does not serve any socially useful function. Its success is due to its ability to circumvent. As a result, he feels that bitcoin should be banned for good.

The French Nobel laureate in economics Jean Tirole warns against bitcoin, stating that it is "an asset without intrinsic value", "without economic reality". He is dubious in terms of two criteria: is it a viable currency in the long term? Does it contribute to the common good? Regarding viability, Jean Tirole is particularly critical of the Initial coin offering (ICO) of three billion dollars in 2017. Advertised as an instrument of financial disintermediation, according to him ICOs neglect the fundamentals of finance. In fact, the use of reliable and well-capitalized intermediaries to monitor projects is fundamental to ensure everything is done correctly. For the economist, the social role of Bitcoin is "elusive". Bitcoins are concentrated in private hands, particularly for fraud and tax evasion.

Bill Gates (ex-CEO of Microsoft), Jack Dorsay (CEO of Twitter), Richard Branson, Chamath Palihapitiy (co-founder of Facebook), the Winklevoss brothers and a series of other billionaires see bitcoin as inevitable.

Jean-Marc Sylvestre, French journalist for the business press, predicts a crash by highlighting its success among those who make dirty money in the drug trade, the illicit guns trade and in international prostitution as well as among populations of emerging countries, who do not have a bank account but are equipped with a smartphone. To this can be added the key role of bitcoin in ransomware attacks, with ransomware often demanding payment in this currency, which is difficult to trace.

As you can see, there are different opinions on Bitcoin and its validity as a currency. Actually, we believe it to be more like digital gold, which is the same idea shared by Michael Saylor, CEO of Microstrategy, and Elon Musk.
In the next chapters we are going to discuss the technical aspects you need to know if you want to buy bitcoin and store it in a safe way.

Chapter 12

Buying Bitcoin

The turnover regarding virtual currencies is constantly increasing, as evidenced by the interest of users on cryptocurrency exchanges. Even if Bitcoin is the best known worldwide, it does not mean that it is the only cryptocurrency to be bought or sold.

Choosing the best cryptocurrency exchange is essential, especially in consideration of the total invested capital value. In fact, there are risks associated with cryptocurrency investing, one of these refers precisely to the choice of the exchange.

Before listing the best exchange sites for buying and selling cryptocurrencies, we will explain in detail what an exchange is and how it works. Therefore, we will focus on the most advantageous solutions on the market today, available to experienced investors and users who are entering the digital currency sector only now.

Cryptocurrency exchanges

Cryptocurrency exchanges are platforms where coins can be exchanged. The most common exchange takes place between dollars or euros for the corresponding value of a virtual currency. For example, if you want to buy one BTC, you will need $58,000 (the present value of a single BTC) plus the commission value for the exchange.

Once the exchange is complete, the newly acquired cryptocurrency must be deposited in a wallet (electronic wallet). The wallet can be compared to a bank account, with which, however, one only has the opportunity to withdraw, deposit or send part or all of the cryptocurrency to another digital wallet or exchange.

The wallet

Each wallet is assigned a specific address, which could be compared to the bank account number code of traditional checking accounts. In addition, a secret key is needed to log into the electronic wallet for the first time. You can then set a login password and encrypt the data.

There are three types of wallets.

- **Software Wallet.** A program downloaded to a computer or mobile device. They are generally among the wallets that guarantee greater security.

- **Online Wallet.** Digital wallets that can be accessed from the Internet through a private key, most often managed by the exchange. Of the three types it is the least safe.

- **Hardware Wallet**. A physical device (most often a USB stick) that makes it possible to access the wallet only if it is connected to a second device. Among all it is the one that offers the greatest safety.

We will talk more about cryptocurrency wallets in a dedicated chapter.

As there are different wallets, there are also different types of exchanges.

- **Exchange fiat to crypto.** They allow you to exchange a fiat currency (e.g. dollar or euro) for a virtual currency.

- **Exchange with centralized management**. Platforms managed by a third party. The positive aspects include the speed of transactions and the low commissions compared to those requested by exchanges for decentralized cryptocurrencies. Among the disadvantages, however, there is a greater risk of running into a scam.

- **Exchange with decentralized management.** The processes are automated, as everything is delegated to the blockchain technology. Consequently, an exchange of this type operates in total safety. However, it is also true that transactions are slower. Furthermore, the variety of cryptocurrencies is still small compared to the offer of other exchanges.

The last aspect to emphasize concerns the commissions, charged to users who operate within the exchange platforms. Broadly speaking, there are four different fees.

- Storage fee;
- Withdrawal fee;
- Order taker fee;
- Order maker fee.

Usually, the fees are inversely proportional to the volumes traded on a monthly basis. This means that higher volumes correspond to lower fees, while when volumes are low, fees tend to rise.

Therefore, if we want to summarize the concepts expressed so far, the choice of an exchange rather than another should be based on the analysis of three important aspects.

- **Safety**. As far as possible, opting for a decentralized exchange platform would be the best decision, but it is also true that it is a rather recent solution with the limitations described above (low speed of operations and few cryptocurrencies to trade).

- **Strategy**. Before choosing an exchange instead of another, you should have already outlined a plan. In this regard, it is important to understand if you want to aim for a fiat-to-crypto exchange or an exchange where only virtual currencies exist.

- **Commissions**. An analysis of the costs to be incurred for the future operations that will be carried out is very important to make a final choice, taking into account the other two factors as well.

The best cryptocurrency exchanges

The list of the best cryptocurrency exchanges features long-lived platforms such as Coinbase Pro, Kraken and Bitstamp, in addition to the more modern Binance. Below we offer a brief presentation of each trading platform, listing pros and cons.

Binance

Binance is the largest international cryptocurrency exchange. Created only in 2017, in a short time it managed to gain the interest of virtual currency traders.

Binance has also recently created its own cryptocurrency (Binance Coin, ticker symbol: BNB). Currently BNB is in the top ten positions of the CoinmarketCap ranking, dominated by Bitcoin and Ethereum.

Until recently, traders on Binance could only trade cryptocurrencies with other cryptocurrencies.

Recently, however, the possibility of exchanging virtual currencies in exchange for fiat currencies has also been introduced.

The main advantages are that there are over 130 cryptocurrencies available and the commissions are around 0.1%. The only disadvantage is that the graphic interface is not very beginner friendly. In fact, we found that people that are just starting out in cryptocurrency find it difficult to navigate through the many possibilities of the site. It is the Ferrari of cryptocurrency exchanges: if you want to buy bitcoin for the first time you do not need a Ferrari.

Wirex

Wirex is a digital payment platform, and an FCA-licensed electronic money institution in the United Kingdom, with a clear mission: to cancel the differences between real and virtual money and make the use of cryptocurrencies easier and more accessible to everyone.

Thanks to the innovative mobile app and the new generation Wirex multi-currency card, the user can buy, exchange and hold a wide range of fiat coins and cryptocurrencies (including BTC, ETH, LTC, XRP, XLM, WXT, WAVES, DAI and NANO) and also spend them in physical stores. All this quickly, safely and without commission. There are many advantages of having a Wirex account, from unlimited access to OTC rates for cryptocurrency exchanges, to new generation rewards.

Services offered and benefits

- **Currency exchange without commission**. Users can exchange fiat and cryptocurrencies instantly on the app for free and at favorable exchange rates.

- **Wirex multi-currency card.** This allows users to spend cryptocurrencies and fiat money wherever Mastercard and Visa are accepted, and participate in the first cryptocurrency cashback program in the world (Cryptoback) to get up to 2% of the cost for each purchase made.

- Free ATM withdrawals up to $500 per month and no monthly fee.

Among the advantages offered by Wirex there are also the free account setup and card issuance and the absence of commissions on card transactions in stores. Furthermore, users have the possibility of recharging the account without restrictions up to 50,000 dollars per transaction by bank transfer.

Sign up process and verification

To register, you need to connect to the website or download the app available for free on the App Store and Play Store. The registration procedure is quick and easy: just fill out the form and click on the link received in the confirmation email.

The verification process takes only a few minutes. You will have to upload the documents to verify your identity and, once verified, set a password for greater security. And speaking of security, to protect its users' data from possible hacker attacks and violation of privacy, Wirex uses SSL (Secure Sockets Layer) technology for all communications between servers and web browsers, which guarantees data protection. Furthermore, two-factor authentication and BitGo's multi-signature technology, which makes it impossible to transfer money without the transaction being authorized with signature by all parties involved. Finally, the platform does not keep payment card numbers, expiration dates or CVV codes. It is a very nice app for buying your first bitcoin, we recommend it.

Coinbase Pro

Coinbase Pro is the world's best known cryptocurrency exchange. It is based in San Francisco and also appears in the ranking of the longest-lived platforms (the year of Coinbase's foundation dates back to 2012).

Compared to other exchanges, there are few cryptocurrencies available for trading in Coinbase Pro. The updated list features Bitcoin, Bitcoin Cash,

Ethereum, Litecoin, EOS, Stellar, Ethereum Classic, Ox and the stablecoin USD Coin (USDC). The possibility of exchanging virtual currencies with fiat currencies should be noted.

Another important aspect to take into consideration when talking about Coinbase Pro is the ease of use of the platform, which is also valid for those who are new to cryptocurrency trading.

Kraken

Kraken was born in 2011, a year earlier than Coinbase. It owes its popularity to the rich fiat currency exchange section for Bitcoin (users can choose between euro, dollar, pound, yen, etc.).

The Kraken exchange currently supports 17 cryptocurrencies. These include Bitcoin, Bitcoin Cash, Bitcoin SV, Ethereum, Ethereum Classic, Ripple, Litecoin, Moreno, EOS, ZCash, DASH, Dogecoin and the stablecoin Tether.

Among the negative sides of Kraken we can mention the arbitrary closure of some accounts managed by normal users, as witnessed by some traders who spoke controversially about the platform founded by Jesse Powell almost ten years ago.

The availability of cryptocurrencies is greater than CoinbasePro, and the ability to exchange fiat currencies for virtual currencies is what makes it attractive for new crypto enthusiasts. However, the slower speed of operations compared to other equally famous exchanges and a question mark on security in light of the complaint relating to the arbitrary closure of some accounts does not give us the confidence to suggest it to those just starting out in crypto.

Bitstamp

Bitstamp was founded in the same year as Kraken (2011) by the very young Nejc Kodrič and Damijan Merlak. Born in 1989, Kodrič created Bitstamp at the age of 22. The exchange, whose base today is in

Luxembourg, was created as a European alternative to Mt. Gox, the historic cryptocurrency exchange site that failed in 2014 (until a few months earlier it held 70% of Bitcoin transactions globally).

One of the main features of Bitstamp is the lower commission value compared to other competitors. For example, the commission on an international bank transfer is 0.05%, while for a withdrawal, 0.09% is the requested fee.

However, like CoinbasePro, Bitstamp does not allow traders to trade a large number of cryptocurrencies. At the moment, exchanges of Bitcoin, Bitcoin Cash, Litecoin, Ethereum and Ripple are allowed.

Bittrex

Bittrex is among the 5 best cryptocurrency exchanges along with the most well-known platforms mentioned so far. Its base is in Seattle, in the United States of America, and this makes Bittrex one of the safest exchanges for traders (in Washington State, security is a central theme in the debate related to the management of virtual currencies).

On Bittrex, only the exchange between cryptocurrencies is allowed, therefore it is not the ideal choice for those who instead aim to exchange between fiat and virtual currencies. The cost of commissions should also be emphasized, the percentage of which on average reaches 0.25%.

Based on its structure, Bittrex is also the platform where the largest number of cryptocurrencies are present. The list also includes Bitcoin, Ethereum, Ripple and Cardano.

Our insight into the best cryptocurrency exchange sites ends here. We remind you that new exchanges are born every day, but we advise you to just use the ones mentioned in this chapter. In fact, the cryptocurrency world is famous for the huge number of scams. Be cautious and everything will be fine.

Chapter 13

Storing your Bitcoin

Now that you have learned where to buy your first bitcoin, it is time to store it properly. In fact, once the purchase is complete you do not want to leave your coins on an exchange. By now you should know that if you do not own the private key, you cannot say you actually own your bitcoins. Therefore, it is important to have a reliable place where you store and accumulate your coins for the future.

In this chapter we are going to take a look at some of the most entrusted cryptocurrency wallets. Let's start with the one we personally use to store our bitcoins: the Ledger Nano X

Ledger Nano X

In the next few pages we will consider all the important aspects to know, including the price of the Ledger Nano X. We will also see how to use it to keep your cryptocurrencies safe, keeping them offline in a device that completely protects them from any cyber attack. This system, we remind you, is the only one that is truly reliable: the online wallets of exchanges, even the most famous ones, are connected to the internet and are consequently exposed to cyber attacks.

Hardware wallets, on the other hand, only connect when you need to perform operations and remain completely inaccessible for the rest of the time. In addition to not being able to be attacked from the outside, hardware wallets also protect you against the possibility that you lose your device.

Thanks to a password system that identifies you in a unique way, in fact, if you lose your Ledger Nano X you just need to buy another one and recover all your virtual currency assets.

The device is even more compact and lighter than the previous ones, with its just 34 grams of weight that make it more pocketable than a normal USB stick. The package includes the following.

- The device;
- A USB cable for connecting it to a computer or smartphone
- The illustrated sheet with instructions for using the Ledger Nano X;
- A strap to hang the device and possibly carry it around the neck;
- Three sheets for recovering passwords, with space to mark them and instructions in case of loss.

As you may imagine, nothing is missing in this top tier product. Ledger puts us in a position to learn how to use the device directly thanks to the instructions in the package and moreover it gives us all the tools to connect it to our electronic devices.

The soul of Ledger Nano X is BOLOS, the operating system developed by Ledger. The code is not open source, which means it cannot be customized by developers but it is also not accessible to possible attackers looking for bugs.

The company jealously guards every string of the BOLOS code, and indeed this intuition has proved very useful over the years for the security of its devices. BOLOS is already installed in the Nano X microchip, so there is no need to do any external installation by downloading to the computer and passing the software via USB cable.

This step, foreseen by some competing products, on the one hand allows everyone to download the firmware versions they prefer; on the other hand, unnecessarily exposing the hardware wallet to an internet connection increases the risk of compromise.

Ledger Nano X is compatible with computers running Windows 8 or later, and Apple devices running Mac iOS 10.9 or later. It also connects to mobile devices. In particular, you need Android 7.0 and iOS 9 to establish a successful connection.
Wanting to draw a dividing line, we can say that it is compatible with all operating systems released or updated after 2017. In any case we recommend that you check the characteristics of the system installed on your device to make sure it is compatible with Ledger Nano X.

Ledger Nano X can connect to your devices in two ways. First of all, as every other hardware walled, it is able to do this via USB cable. The novelty of this year, however, is the possibility of connecting the Ledger to your devices via Bluetooth as well.

When the company announced this feature, disputes immediately flared up. Bluetooth connections, in fact, are much easier to attack than those via the internet. If the device is already designed to stay connected to the network for the shortest possible time, the possibility of leaving it connected to Bluetooth for hours does not seem very coherent with the philosophy of cryptocurrencies.

However, Ledger has confirmed that the data transmitted via Bluetooth are public ones. This means that, even if stolen by someone, it cannot be useful in any way; all private cryptographic keys are unique and jealously guarded within the wallet, and never leave the device. When connected via Bluetooth or USB cable to a device, the Ledger Nano X acts like a piggy bank that can be used to receive or send cryptocurrencies.

Obviously, each device must be configured using dedicated software and personal passwords, so that even in the event of theft, no one can connect it to their computer and use it at will. Even in this case, however, the connected device remains shielded thanks to the dedicated application that filters the passage of information.

Thanks to this intermediation, all critical data is never transmitted outside the Nano X.

The new Ledger is compatible with over 1,100 cryptocurrencies, and software updates gradually widen the range of options. Despite this, only 100 types of different cryptocurrencies can be stored for each Nano X. While it is rare to find someone who needs to store more than 100 different crypto, it is still a limitation for some people who like to diversify their portfolios and act as a venture capitalist for cryptocurrencies.

To add a cryptocurrency, simply open the Ledger Live software from any device. Once the program is open, you will be asked to authenticate using your credentials, thus accessing the main panel with all the available functions. At this point you will have to go to the catalog of available crypto, choosing the one you are interested in adding to our wallet.

Once the application has been selected, its download will begin. The code will be transferred to your Ledger Nano X which, from that moment on, will be ready to host wallets of the selected cryptocurrency. To add your portfolio you will have to open the application and complete the process. You will be asked for the access keys to your wallet, and once this is done we will have correctly configured the storage on our device.

What is important to understand is that, technically, cryptocurrencies are not "sent" to the Ledger, as they are not transferred from one wallet to another. The only thing that changes is the information on the blockchain that says where those funds are kept.

In any case, for simplicity, we will continue to use the term "send" to make the subject clearer. Once you open the application, suppose it is that of Bitcoin, at the top you will find two buttons: "Send" and "Receive".

By clicking on "Receive" you will display a unique code that can be used as a destination address for sending your Bitcoins directly to the Ledger Nano X. At this point it will be sufficient to use this key as the address for sending your cryptocurrencies.

The procedure for sending varies depending on where you previously stored your tokens; if you buy them for the first time from an exchange, you can have them sent directly to the address that appears on the Ledger Nano X.

The procedure for sending cryptocurrencies is almost similar to the previous one, with the only difference that you will have to click on the "Send" button instead of the "Receive" button. Your offline wallet will ask you for the recipient wallet. Once entered, just click on the "Send" button to complete the procedure.

Thanks to the cryptocurrency applications on Ledger Nano X you have the ability to check your balance and your incoming and outgoing transactions at any time. In this way you can always have an overview of your assets and keep cash flows under control.

There are various online stores that sell the Ledger, but it becomes extremely important to be able to trust the retailer. Someone, in fact, could sell compromised devices with the aim of stealing the coins contained inside. In fact, it is sufficient to update the operating system and install one with specially written code, to achieve this malicious effect.

If you don't want to take any chances, we recommend you to buy it directly on the Ledger website (https://www.ledger.com/).

Trezor

Trezor is a hardware wallet that connects to your computer via USB port. It can stock, send and receive cryptocurrencies of different types, among which we can mention Bitcoin, Ethereum, Ethereum Classic,

Litecoin, Namecoin, Dogecoin, Dash, Bitcoin Testnet and even ZCash.

It includes important security features, such as a password manager and also a two-step authentication. It can also be integrated with other very popular wallets, such as MyEtherWallet and Copay, to securely manage even the virtual wallets that you may have opened on these specific platforms.

Trezor is a hardware wallet with an essential design, small in size, easy to connect to your PC and which also comes with a small band that allows you to connect it directly to your keychain, making it even more comfortable to be carried around.

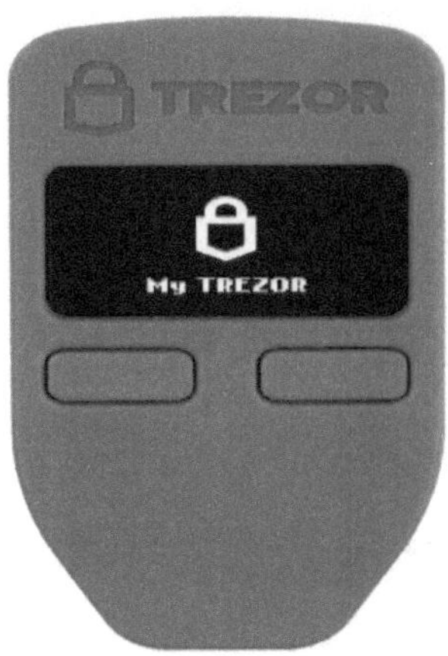

At the time of writing it is available in two different colors: black and white. On the front of the device you will also find a low resolution white on black display and the two buttons that you will need to go on with the operations or to cancel them.

It is also possible to interact with all or almost all of the major exchanges on the internet thanks to the software that is delivered together with the hardware wallet and above all thanks to the Google Chrome extension that Trezor makes available.

Trezor offers certainly adequate security with respect to the management of wallets that contain important quantities of cryptocurrency within them. First of all, it allows you to have a backup of the wallet with a 24-word passphrase that is generated during the installation phase. After the first installation, a PIN code must also be entered: any mistake in entering the PIN exponentially increases the waiting time for the next try. It means that it would take about 17 years to make 30 attempts.

With the 24-word passphrase it is possible to recover the wallet at any time, even if the trezor we bought should be lost or destroyed. Equally important to take into account is the possibility of integrating the recovery methods even with virtual wallets such as Electrum. This is a feature the Ledger Nano X does not have.

Another important security feature concerning Trezor is the fact that to approve a transaction the keys on the hardware wallet must necessarily be pushed. This means that even in the very unlikely case that someone should enter your Trezor remotely, they will not be able to approve transactions without your consent.

The privacy profile for TREZOR is also interesting. In fact, we are faced with a device that has no serial code and therefore cannot be traced by anyone, much less by the manufacturer. This is a huge advantage in a world, that of cryptocurrencies, where user tracking is unfortunately a reality for almost every type of service that you can use.

Once you have purchased it, nobody will be able to associate your Trezor with your order. It is also worth mentioning that Trezor is also compatible with the large of the most popular software wallets in the world, among which we can mention Electrum, GreenAddress, Multibit, Mycelium and also with the software wallet offered by myTREZOR.com

It is also worth remembering what the technical specifications are as communicated by the manufacturer.

- Weight: 12 grams
- Size: 6 x 3 x 0.6 cm
- CPU: ARM Cortex M3 at 120 MHz
- Display: 128 × 64 pixel OLED Bright
- Connectivity: Micro USB
- Supported systems: Windows, Mac, Linux, Android

Furthermore, the Trezor source code is available on github, with the parent company inviting anyone with interest and ability to modify the code and to propose the aforementioned changes to the mother line of the firmware code as well.

This is a great opportunity for those who would like to know more about cryptocurrencies and programming even on an exquisitely more technical level. If for whatever reason you do not want to get a Ledger Nano X, then the Trezor is definitely the second best hardware wallet there is right now.

Chapter 14

The Proof of Keys Day

As we have seen in the previous chapter, keeping your private keys safe is essential to ensure financial independence. Unfortunately, many cryptocurrency investors entrust their money exclusively to exchanges. This practice is far from safe, considering that exchanges have full control over cryptocurrency deposits.

Since the early days of Bitcoin, billions have been lost due to scams and cyberattacks against exchanges. The hack of the Mt.Gox exchange in 2014 is one of the most famous and controversial cases, and is still under investigation today.

The idea for the Proof of Keys was created by Trace Mayer, a podcaster and cryptocurrency investor. He

created the concept as an annual celebration with the aim of encouraging investors to reclaim their monetary autonomy.
As discussed above, many people leave their cryptocurrencies on exchanges. This practice is inherently dangerous as these exchanges have full control over the private keys of the deposit addresses.

In this context, the Proof of Keys day aims to prevent investors from relying on exchanges for storing their cryptocurrencies. The concept is often presented with a short but effective motto: not your keys, not your Bitcoin.

The first Proof of Keys day took place on January 3rd, 2019 - the day of the 10th anniversary of the genesis block on the Bitcoin network.
In other words, Proof of Keys day celebrates financial sovereignty. Its goal is to encourage cryptocurrency investors to move their funds from exchanges to personal wallets. By taking full control over our private keys, we are assured that no one but us can access our funds.

Results of the Proof of Keys day

The philosophy behind the Proof of Keys day is perfectly in line with that of Bitcoin. By replacing third-party intermediaries with a trustless system for the transfer of value, individuals can confidently cooperate with each other - without giving up their monetary autonomy.

New investors learn how to move their coins

Cryptocurrency investors should be comfortable moving cryptocurrencies from place to place. While this may seem simple to some, beginners often find it difficult to understand the different types of wallets and how to use them.

For this, the Proof of Keys day encourages investors to learn more about the different types of crypto wallets and to practice their use. It is also a reminder of how value is transferred within decentralized blockchain networks.

Remind investors who really owns the private keys

As already mentioned, the central mission set by Trace Mayer at the origin of the Proof of Keys day was to encourage every cryptocurrency investor to own their own private keys. Leaving cryptocurrencies on an exchange means you have zero control over your own funds.

Even if it only happens once a year, Proof of Keys day is an opportunity for every investor to take control of their funds. While this day is a great warning about who owns what, it means very little if investors don't go all out in protecting their coins.

Unmasking shady or dishonest exchanges

Financial institutions are famous for the practice known as fractional reserve. In essence, it is a system that allows institutions to leverage existing deposits by lending more money than they actually own.

Unfortunately, this is risky for the depositor, as a "bank run" could lead to bankruptcy.
In the context of the crypto sector, Proof of Keys day can encourage thousands of investors to withdraw their funds from exchanges. If a large percentage of investors decide to do this on the same day, they could eventually reveal exchanges that practice fractional reserve methods or are lying about their reserves.

Fortunately, the transparency of Bitcoin and other blockchain networks offers exchanges a very simple way to make their funds publicly verifiable.

Celebrating the genesis block of Bitcoin

Last but not least, Proof of Keys day is a way to celebrate the first block mined on the Bitcoin network. This block is known as the genesis block. The genesis block contains the first Bitcoin transaction made, in which Satoshi Nakamoto sent 50 BTC to Hal Finney.
Another memorable transaction took place on May 22nd, 2010, when two pizzas were bought for 10,000

bitcoins. The episode is now known as the Bitcoin Pizza day.

How to participate in the Proof of Keys movement

It doesn't matter if you are a newcomer or a veteran in the field of cryptocurrencies. Taking part in the Proof of Keys day is very simple. As we have already said, the idea is to declare financial autonomy by withdrawing all funds from exchanges (or other third party services).

First of all, you can take an inventory of all the funds you own on cryptocurrency exchanges. This will give you an idea of who really owns what when it comes to your bitcoins and altcoins.

Then, find a cryptocurrency wallet that you are comfortable with. In addition to ease of use, it is important to consider the security level of each type of wallet before making your choice. Finally, send your funds to your personal wallet to own and control your private keys.

Some people participate in the Proof of Keys movement once a year, moving funds off exchanges for one day on January 3rd to celebrate and affirm their financial sovereignty.

This practice is common among active traders, who must hold funds on exchanges in order to trade. Then, after the celebration, they move the funds back to exchanges. However, long-term investors who do not trade in the short or medium term should keep funds on a personal wallet until they decide to sell their coins.

Proof of Keys day is a simple but important event that reminds cryptocurrency investors who really owns their private keys. Millions of crypto enthusiasts join the celebration, moving funds off exchanges to their personal wallets.

As the blockchain industry grows, events like Proof of Keys day will not only help educate the community on the importance of private key ownership, but also on security principles in general.

Chapter 15

Bitcoin Futures

In the previous chapters we always talked about buying "physical" bitcoins. However, the financial world is incredibly fascinating and has the ability to create financial instruments that are extremely complex and have no direct contact with "reality". Since this book is about Bitcoin, we feel it is extremely important to talk about the less known possibilities you have to interact with this asset. Therefore, in the next few pages we are going to cover everything you need to know about futures.

Many people are wondering how bitcoin futures work. From a strictly technical point of view, these are normal futures contracts, as they have been in the financial markets for a long time. Their peculiarity lies in the fact that they have BTC as an underlying asset.

In fact, futures contracts are precisely contracts between two parties for the purchase or sale of goods at a future date, or on expiration, and at a specific price agreed between the parties themselves. Upon expiry of the contract, the parties are in fact obliged to honor the agreements, buying and selling at the previously agreed price, regardless of whether the price of the underlying asset may have decreased or increased in the meantime.

They are used as a kind of insurance against the risks of price fluctuations. However, very often they are used to speculate as well. They are also exchangeable, i.e. once a futures contract has been issued it can be sold on the market by the parties who have signed it. When a futures contract is signed between two parties, one agrees to buy and the other agrees to sell. Those who decide to buy the underlying are said to open a long position, while those who decide to sell are said to open a short position.

Futures contracts were created specifically for the exchange of commodities, but in fact they can be used to trade any asset, including purely financial assets, such as bitcoin or other cryptocurrencies.

Bitcoin futures can be used to protect yourself from significant fluctuations in the value of BTC, but in reality very often they are used to speculate on the price of BTC without actually owning the coins.

Furthermore, many exchanges that allow BTC trading are not fully regulated, while those that allow BTC futures trading, such as ICE or CME, are fully regulated. Futures allow trading even for those who do not trust unregulated exchanges, or those institutional investors who simply cannot invest in markets that are not fully regulated.

Each single contract contains a certain volume of the underlying asset, and in the case of bitcoin futures this volume is usually 1 BTC. There are also futures contracts based on physical bitcoins, such as those of Bakkt, and others based on indexes that replicate the price, such as those of the CME.

Those not based on physical bitcoins are settled in cash, i.e. at maturity the exchange takes place in normal fiat currencies, and not in BTC. Since the first bitcoin futures contracts were placed on the market in December 2017, their success has gradually grown, so much so that the trading volumes in recent periods have begun to be significant.

Indeed, to tell the truth on those platforms where it is possible to exchange both physical bitcoins and bitcoin futures contracts, the trading volumes of the latter tend to significantly exceed those of real BTC exchanges, precisely because of the characteristics peculiar to futures, which allow very easy exchanges and within the reach of even the most demanding investors. This is a feature that is not only valid in the bitcoin market, but also in those of other commodities. However, remember that when you are trading futures, you never own the actual underlying asset.

What makes futures so speculative is the possibility to use leverage. Let's discover what it is and what it involves.

Leverage

Leverage is a tool that allows you to increase exposure on a financial market for a relatively modest capital investment. It is undoubtedly one of the most important features of trading with futures. When you invest in a leveraged product, the exchange will ask you to deposit only a small portion of the total position value. The remaining part of the capital will be made available by the exchange itself.

However, your profit or loss will be based on the entire exposure. So the amount you gain or lose may seem very high compared to the capital actually invested. It may even exceed your initial investment. This is the key concept of leverage and what attracts most cryptocurrency enthusiasts.

The initial outlay is called the margin or deposit requirement. Your provider will require it to cover, in whole or in part, any losses you could potentially incur. The margin is usually a small part of the entire exposure and its value depends on various factors. For instance, a more liquid and less volatile market requires a lower margin (eg 5%) than a volatile and less liquid market.

Some products require fixed margins per single contract, while in other cases the margin is calculated as a percentage of the position value.

How leverage works

Let's start with an example that clarifies doubts. If a particular market requires a margin of 10%, it means that by investing only 100 dollars you can get exposure on an investment of 1000 dollars. The leverage is therefore equal to 10 times the value you invested or, as they say in technical jargon, the leverage is 10:1.

Suppose you want to buy 1 bitcoin futures contract. If the current price is 60 euro, the transaction would cost you 60,000 dollars. If the price rises by 2000 dollars per contract, you can close your position at 62,000 dollars.

However, some exchanges offer you the opportunity to buy the shares of a bitcoin futures contract using leverage, simply by paying a margin (i.e. a percentage of the entire sum of 6000 dollars) in exchange for a total exposure.

Let's say the initial margin requirement is 10%. You will pay 10% x 60000 dollars x 1 contract = 6000 dollars. And if the share price were to rise from $60,000 to $62,000 you would make the same profit ($2000) as a non-leveraged transaction.

You made the same profit in both cases, but using leverage you only had to shell out a deposit of $6000 instead of the full $60,000. Your return was 100%, far greater than the 20% you would have achieved by buying the contract directly.

Although leverage is an excellent financial tool, it is still advisable to always remember that it amplifies not only the potential profits but also the losses, which can sometimes even exceed the initial deposit in the event that the market moves significantly against you.

Benefits of leverage

The main advantage of leverage is that it allows you to keep more liquidity in your portfolio, as you only have to tie up a small portion of the capital. You can also make the most of your capital and perhaps invest in a number of different assets rather than just one or two, diversifying your portfolio. However, it should be remembered that by operating with leverage you renounce all the advantages deriving from the actual ownership of bitcoin. It is also essential to remember that you may be required to pay additional margin to cover your losses should the market move in a direction that is unfavorable to you.

Who should use leverage

Investors and traders use leverage to amplify their exposure to various markets. This allows them to keep more liquidity in their portfolios to devote to other investments, diversifying their capital better than they could have done by physically purchasing the assets. You can use leverage on most cryptocurrencies on Binance.

Companies also use leverage to invest in assets from which to derive a relatively high return. A popular business strategy is to use debt to finance assets. This is because companies believe they can derive from these investments more than the cost of the interest they have to pay on their debt.

The effect of financial leverage

You must always bear in mind that leverage amplifies the scope of both gains and losses. While you have a good chance of making substantial profits, your potential losses are not limited to the initial deposit. The maximum loss, expressed as a percentage of the investment, is higher when you trade with leverage. However, it should be noted that the maximum risk, i.e. the highest amount you could lose, is the same whether you buy the assets for their full value or pay only a margin.

It is therefore important that you think in terms of the total position value and not just the margin you anticipated. You should therefore not make a leveraged investment without being prepared to fully cover any losses.

6 Advantages of Bitcoin futures

According to some experts, trading with Bitcoin futures could also be the best way to bet on the most widespread cryptocurrency in the world. Here are the six main reasons why some believe this to be the case.

1. **Futures exchanges are managed by market experts**

The creators of Bitcoin invented the blockchain, a cutting-edge technology that promises to revolutionize the world. However, they are not experts in creating markets. The CME and the CBOE both have a long experience in creating futures contracts for buying and selling. The launch of these trading venues will improve price management. This means that any new Bitcoin information will be quickly reflected on the contract price.

2. **Large financial companies are familiar with futures**

Wall Street firms are familiar with futures exchanges and how they work. Most of these carry out back-office operations that allow you to easily trade such instruments. This ease of use will attract more dollar volume on Bitcoin-related contracts. As a result, the Bitcoin futures market will become very liquid, perhaps more liquid than Bitcoin itself. For instance the SPDR S&P500 ETF is more traded than the underlying stocks in the index and a similar dynamic could also occur on Bitcoin futures.

3. **The reference price**

Contracts will be settled on each trading day using a transparent reference price. The reference price may not be perfect, but it will soon be written in contracts that provide for the payment or receipt of Bitcoin as is the case in other markets. For example, jewelry manufacturers and retailers often use gold reference prices in their contracts. In short, having a transparent settlement price will simplify the issue of using Bitcoin as a payment method.

4. **Futures contracts are not lost**

You can lose money on it, but you will never lose a futures contract. On cryptocurrency exchanges, however, it has already happened that Bitcoins were lost or stolen.

5. **You can bet on the price drop**

Going short on a futures contract is as simple as buying it. Those who believe that the Bitcoin price is in a speculative bubble can thus bet on a deflation of prices.

6. **It is a regulated market**

The Commodity Futures Trading Commission (CFTC) regulates futures trading. Those who love Bitcoin because it is not a government currency will not agree that regulation is an advantage. However, it's a significant plus for Bitcoin fans in general. The good news is that CFTC rules aren't as tough as those for stocks and bonds. What it does is introduce some rules that all market participants must adhere to and sets a level playing field for all speculators and investors who expose themselves to futures contracts. This feature will attract professional traders and thus increase the trading volume in the market. More trading volume will be beneficial for Bitcoin fans because it will make cryptocurrency futures a significant financial instrument, and consequently Bitcoin itself as well.

Chapter 16

Bitcoin Options

Now that you understand the fundamentals of bitcoin futures, we can discuss an even more complex financial instrument. We are talking about options.

So mistreated by retail investors and yet so used by large investors on traditional markets, bitcoin options are a great tool to hedge spot positions.

In this chapter we will try to clarify what they are and we will try to demonstrate that the bad reputation they enjoy in the eyes of the general public is actually unfounded and that on the contrary, if used correctly and consciously, they possess characteristics that make them tools. very useful to enrich your arsenal of investment and trading strategies.

To do this, let's start by clarifying the basic concept, which however many manage to make complicated right from the start.

How do options on Bitcoin work?

The option can actually be considered as an insurance on the asset you hold, Bitcoin in your case, against a particular scenario that you think or fear may occur. To have this possibility, you pay an initial sum (exactly as you pay the insurance premium at the time of stipulation), high or low depending on the probability that the scenario has to come true. And exactly as in the case of an insurance, the option also has an expiry date, at the choice of the purchaser, beyond which it is no longer valid and can be exercised by the holder.

If your vision is a rise in the price of bitcoin, you will buy an upward option that "protects" you from a price increase beyond a certain value and will allow you to buy BTC in the future at a cheaper price (strike price). This type of option is called the CALL option.

If, on the other hand, your view is bearish, you will buy a bearish option that protects you from a decrease in the value of bitcoin below a value of your choice (always called the strike price). This option is called PUT.

And now the question that arises spontaneously: “but if my vision is bullish, why not buy Bitcoin right away before the price goes up? And if it is bearish, why not sell now?"

Well, the advantage of the option is precisely this. It gives you the opportunity to delay the decision to a future moment. If you were right, the insurance / option will make you collect the price difference between the value decided at the time of stipulation and the actual value on the day of sale (or expiry of the option). Otherwise, the option expires and you will have lost the premium paid initially. It should be emphasized that, as in the case of an insurance, the maximum loss is the sum paid on stipulation.

There is no liquidation risk, so much so that no maintenance margin is required for the purchase of options and there is no additional "hidden" outlay in addition to the initial one for the purchase.

Where to buy options

Certainly the first market to be mentioned in this sense is the CME, Chicago Mercantile Exchange, where futures and related options are listed on traditional financial markets. From 2020 the options on Bitcoin have also been added. The same goes for the BAKKT platform which is part of the ICE group. However, trading in these markets is only open to institutional and professional investors. A common investor looking to buy Bitcoin options has to rely on other types of platforms. Almost all exchanges offer the possibility to buy futures, but not options on Bitcoin, whose trading is currently the prerogative of Binance, FTX, Deribit, Okex and LedgerX only.

While as far as futures are concerned, all exchanges provide similar, if not identical, services, for options the situation is different. In fact, Binance and FTX provide a service only on demand, i.e. there is no market with a book consisting of bids and offers such as we are used to seeing, but it is necessary to request a particular option with the desired characteristics and expect a quotation from the exchange itself or from another user of the platform willing to sell it to us.

This type of transaction can be defined as OTC, i.e. each option is tailored to the applicant and is only recommended for expert users who know what they are doing, as this type of market is less liquid and less transparent.

Instead, Deribit, Okex and LedgerX offer a type of negotiation similar to that of any crypto or crypto futures. Therefore, they are standardized, complete with a buy and sell book, and the same characteristics for each market participant. This feature makes buying, selling, and understanding what you are doing much easier.

If you are a beginner, we advise you to stick to the basic strategy of buying and selling spot bitcoins. In fact, futures and options are two extremely complicated financial instruments and should be used only by those that have some trading experience.

Chapter 17

The Best Way to Accumulate Bitcoin

We have already written a book on Bitcoin and cryptocurrency trading, where we encourage readers to master the art of buying high and selling low. This time around, since we are talking to a lot of beginners, we would like to suggest a complementary approach to active trading.

In fact, active trading can be stressful, challenging and still yield poor results. However, there are other options available. Like many investors, you may be looking for a less demanding and time-consuming investment strategy. Or you prefer a more passive investment style. You have many options in the cryptocurrency ecosystem, including staking, lending your assets, participating in mining pools, and more.

But what if you want to invest in the markets but don't know where to start? More precisely, what would be the optimal way to develop a long-term position? In this chapter, we will discuss an investment strategy known as a DCA, or dollar cost averaging, which offers an easy way to mitigate some of the risks involved in opening a position.

What is DCA?

Dollar cost averaging is an investment strategy that aims to reduce the impact of volatility on the purchase of assets. It consists of buying equal amounts of the asset at regular intervals.

The premise is that by entering the market in this way the investment may be less affected by volatility than entering with a single big purchase. Why? Because buying at regular intervals can level out the average price. In the long run, such a strategy reduces the negative impact a bad income can have on your investment. Let's see how the dollar cost averaging strategy works and why you might want to consider using it.

The advantages of dollar cost averaging

The main benefit of dollar cost averaging is that it reduces the risk of placing a bet at the wrong time. Market timing is among the most difficult elements when it comes to trading or investing. Often, even if the direction of a trade is correct, the timing may be wrong - which makes the whole trade inaccurate. The capital accumulation plan helps mitigate this risk.

If you divide your investment into smaller portions, you are likely to get better results than investing the same amount of money in one block. Making a purchase with bad timing is surprisingly easy, and can lead to less than ideal results. Additionally, you can eliminate some of the preconceptions from your decision-making process. When you rely on dollar cost averaging, the strategy will make the decisions for you.

Dollar cost averaging, of course, does not completely mitigate the risk. The idea is just to make market entry smoother to minimize the risk of wrong timing. Capital accumulation plans are by no means a guarantee of a successful investment - other factors must also be taken into consideration, such as the duration of the investment and the asset you are investing in.

As we have already said, finding the right moment in the market is extremely difficult. Even the greatest veterans of trading sometimes struggle to read the market. Therefore, if you entered a position using the dollar cost averaging strategy, you may also need to consider your exit plan, a trading strategy for exiting the position.

Now, if you've determined a target price (or price range), this can be pretty straightforward. Again, you will need to divide your investment equally and start selling them once the market approaches your target. This way, you can mitigate the risk of not going out at the right time. However, this is entirely up to your individual investing system.

Someone adopts a “buy and hold” strategy, where essentially the goal is never to sell, as the value of the purchased assets is expected to continue to rise over time. Check out the Dow Jones Industrial Average's performance over the past century below.

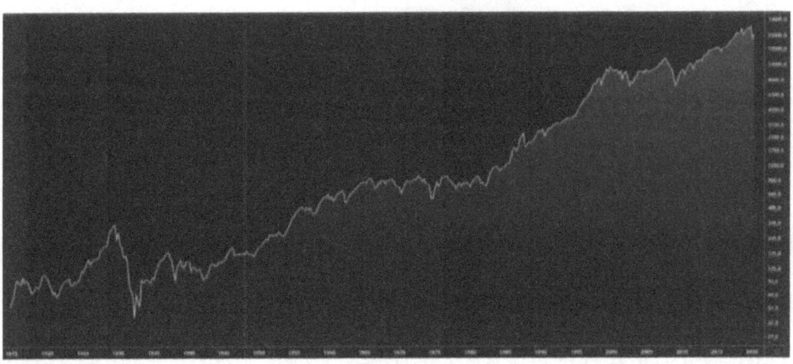

Despite the presence of short periods of recession, the Dow has been in a continuous uptrend. The purpose of a buy and hold strategy is to enter the market and stay in the position long enough to eliminate the importance of timing.

However, it is important to point out that this type of strategy is usually stock market oriented and may not be applicable to cryptocurrency markets. Remember that the Dow's performance correlates with a real-world economy. Other asset classes will perform very differently, especially if they are exclusively supported by speculation. We are not saying that this is the case for Bitcoin. On the contrary, in this case a dollar cost averaging strategy works very well.

Examples of dollar cost averaging strategies

Let's look at this strategy through an example. Let's assume you have a fixed amount of $10,000 dollars, and we think investing in Bitcoin is a reasonable bet. You also believe the price has a good chance of staying in the current zone, which is a good point to build up and develop a position using a dollar cost averaging strategy.

You could split the $10,000 into 100 $100 parts. Every day, you will buy $100 worth of Bitcoin no matter what the price is. In this way, you will distribute your income over a period of approximately three months.

Now, let's try to demonstrate the flexibility of dollar cost averaging with a different plan. Let's assume that Bitcoin has just entered a bear market, and that it will be at least two years before a sustained bull trend. However, you do expect a bull trend eventually, and you would like to prepare in advance.
Should you use the same strategy as before? Probably not. In fact, this investment portfolio has a much longer time horizon. Your $10,000 would remain allocated to this strategy for a few more years. So what's the plan?

You could split the investment back into 100 $100 parts. However, this time around, you will be buying $100 worth of Bitcoin every week. There are around 52 weeks in a year, so the whole strategy will run over a span of nearly two years. In this way, you will develop a long-term position as the downtrend takes its course. You will not lose the train when the uptrend begins, and you have also mitigated some of the risks associated with buying into a downtrend.

Keep in mind that this strategy can be risky when you are buying into a downtrend. For some investors, it would be best to wait for the end of the downtrend to be confirmed to start entering. If they wait, the average cost will likely be higher, but on the other hand many of the downside risks will be mitigated.

Dollar cost averaging calculator

You can find a great calculator for Bitcoin dollar cost averaging plans by visiting www.dcabtc.com. You can specify the amount, the time horizon, the intervals, and get an idea of the progress of various strategies over time. You will see that in the case of Bitcoin, which is in a sustained long-term uptrend, the strategy would have worked consistently.

Below you can see the performance of your investment if you had only bought $10 worth of Bitcoin every week for the past five years. $10 a week doesn't seem like much, does it? In April 2021, you would have invested a total of around $2600, and your bitcoin stack would be worth around $70,000.

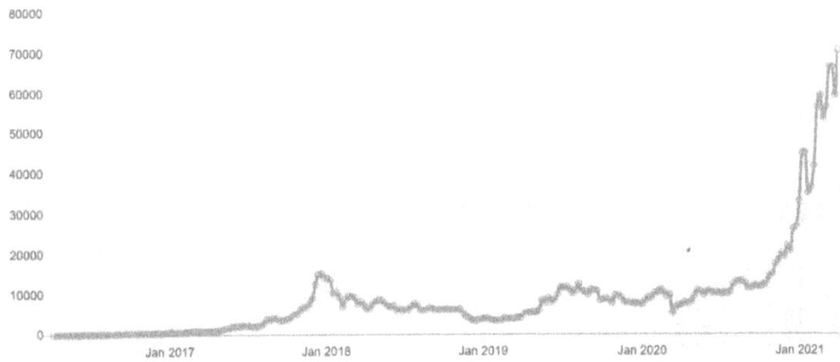
80000
70000
60000
50000
40000
30000
20000
10000
0
Jan 2017
Jan 2018
Jan 2019
Jan 2020
Jan 2021

Chapter 18

Bitcoin as a Store of Value

When we think of a safe asset, precious metals such as gold or silver probably come to mind. They are very popular investments as hedges against turbulence in traditional markets. The debate on Bitcoin's position in the footsteps of these assets is still on. In this chapter, we will look at some of the central arguments for and against Bitcoin as a store of value.

What is a store of value?

A store of value is an asset that can maintain its value over time. If you bought a good store of value today, you could be reasonably certain that its value will not decline over time. Going forward, you would expect the asset to have a similar (if not greater) value.

When you think of a "safe haven" asset of this type, you are likely to imagine gold or silver. There are a few reasons why these have traditionally held their value, which we will look at shortly.

The properties of a good store of value

To understand what the characteristics of a good store of value are, let's first explore those of a bad store of value. If we want to preserve something for long periods of time, it seems logical that it must be durable.

Let's consider food. Apples and bananas have some intrinsic value, as humans have to feed themselves to live. When food is scarce, these products will undoubtedly be very valuable, but that doesn't make them a good store of value. They will be of much less value if we keep them in a safe for several years, as they will obviously degrade.

Instead, let's consider something with an intrinsic value that is also durable, for example pasta. It is better in the long run, but there is still no guarantee that it will hold its value. Pasta is produced at low cost from readily available resources. Anyone can flood the market with new pasta, so pasta in circulation will see its value decrease as supply exceeds demand. Consequently, in order for something to hold value, it must also be scarce.

Some see fiat currencies (dollars, euros, yen) as a valid way to preserve wealth as they hold their long-term value. In reality, they are very bad stores of value because their purchasing power decreases significantly as new units are created (just like pasta). You can take your life savings and hide them under the mattress for twenty years, but they won't have the same purchasing power when you finally decide to spend them.

In the year 2000, with $100,000 you could have bought a lot more than you can today. This is mainly due to inflation, which refers to the increase in the prices of goods and services. In many cases, inflation is caused by an excessive supply of fiat currency resulting from the government's practice of printing new money.

To illustrate this phenomenon, suppose we own 25% of the total supply of $100 billion - hence, $25 billion. Time passes and the government decides to print, for example, another $800 billion to stimulate the economy. Our piece of the pie suddenly dropped to ~3%. There's a lot more money out there now, so it makes sense that our slice doesn't have the same purchasing power as before.

Like the pasta we mentioned earlier, dollars aren't expensive to make. What we have described above can take place within a few days. For a good store of value, it should be difficult to flood the market with new units. In other words, our slice of the pie should dilute very slowly, or not diminish at all. Taking gold as an example, we know that its supply is limited. We also know that it is very difficult to extract. So even if the demand for gold suddenly increases, turning on a printer isn't enough to create more. It must be extracted from the ground, as always. Even as demand grows, supply cannot be materially increased to satisfy it.

Bitcoin as a store of value

Since the early days of Bitcoin, its supporters have put forward the thesis that cryptocurrency is more like "digital gold" than a simple digital currency. In recent years, this narrative has been picked up by many Bitcoin enthusiasts.

The thesis of Bitcoin as a store of value states that this cryptocurrency is one of the most solid assets known to man. Proponents of the thesis believe that Bitcoin is the best way to preserve wealth over time by protecting it from devaluation.

Bitcoin is known for its incredible volatility. It might seem illogical how an asset that can lose 20% of its value in one day may be considered by many to be a store of value. However, even considering its numerous collapses, it remains to this day the best performing asset in history. So why is Bitcoin considered a store of value?

Bitcoin shortage

Perhaps one of the more compelling arguments for the store of value thesis is that Bitcoin has a limited supply. As you may recall from previous chapters, there will never be more than 21 million bitcoins. The protocol guarantees this property with a rule carved into the code.

The only way in which new coins can be created is in the mining process, in some ways analogous to gold mining. However, instead of drilling into the ground, Bitcoin miners must solve a cryptographic puzzle using computational power. By doing so they will earn new coins.

Over time, the reward decreases following events known as halving. As the name suggests, each halving halves the reward. In the early days of Bitcoin, the system distributed 50BTC to every miner that produced a valid block. During the first halving, this number was reduced to 25 BTC. The next halving halved it to 12.5 BTC, and the next one will cut the reward to 6.25 bitcoin per block. This process will continue for another 100+ years until the final fraction of the last coin is in circulation.

Let's create a model similar to the example we did earlier with our fiat currency. Suppose we bought 25% of the supply of Bitcoin (i.e., 5,250,000 coins) many years ago. When we acquired these coins, we knew our percentage would stay the same as there is no entity capable of adding more coins to the system. There is no government here - or rather, not in the traditional sense (more details soon). So, if we had bought 25% of the maximum supply in 2010, we would still have 25% today.

Decentralization

Maybe you are thinking, it is only open-source software. Everyone can copy the code and create their own version with 100 million more coins.

In fact, you could. Let's say you can clone the software, make the changes and run a node. Everything seems to work. There is only one problem, though: there are no other nodes to connect to. You see, as soon as you

changed your software parameters, the members of the Bitcoin network started ignoring you. You have forked, and the program you are running is no longer what is globally accepted as Bitcoin.
What you just did is functionally the equivalent of taking a picture of the Mona Lisa and claiming that there are now two Mona Lisa. You can convince yourself that this is the case, but good luck convincing someone else.

We mentioned that there is some kind of government in Bitcoin. This government is made up of each user running the software. The only way the protocol can be changed is with the majority accepting the changes.

Getting a majority to add coins would be no easy feat - after all, you're asking them to devalue their own funds. At present, even seemingly insignificant features take years to reach consensus across the network.

As it grows and gets bigger and bigger, promoting changes will get harder and harder. Therefore, holders can be reasonably sure that the supply will not be inflated. Even though the software is man-made, the decentralization of the network means that Bitcoin acts more as a natural resource than as code that can be arbitrarily modified.

The properties of good currencies

Proponents of the store-of-value thesis also point out characteristics of Bitcoin that make it a good currency. It is not only a limited digital resource, it also shares characteristics that have traditionally been adopted in the various currencies of history for centuries.

Gold has been used as a currency by several civilizations since their inception. There are several reasons behind this choice. We have already talked about durability and scarcity. These properties can create good assets, but not necessarily good forms of money. For this, fungibility, portability and divisibility are needed.

Fungibility

Fungibility means that the units are indistinguishable. With gold, you can take any two ounces, and they will have the same value. This also applies to things like stocks and cash. It doesn't matter which particular unit you own - it will have the same value as any other of the same type.

Bitcoin's fungibility is a thorny topic. It shouldn't matter which coin you own. In most cases, 1 BTC = 1 BTC. Things get complicated when we consider that each unit can be linked to previous transactions. There are cases where companies blacklist funds they believe have been involved in criminal activity, even if the holder received them later.

Should it matter? It is difficult to understand why. When you are paying for something with a banknote, neither you nor the merchant know what it was used for three transactions ago. There is no concept of a transaction history - new banknotes have no more value than used ones.

At worst, it is possible that older bitcoins (with a longer history) will sell for less than new bitcoins. Depending on who you ask, this hypothesis could be the biggest threat to Bitcoin or something you don't need to worry about. For now, however, Bitcoin is functionally fungible. There have only been a few isolated incidents involving frozen coins due to a historical suspicion.

Portability

Portability denotes the ease of transportation of an asset. $10,000 in $100 bills? Rather easy to move. $10,000 oil equivalent? A little less.

Sound money must have a small form factor. It must be easy to transport to allow individuals to pay each other for goods and services. Gold has traditionally been excellent in this area. At the time of writing, a standard gold coin holds a value of nearly $ 1,500. Many purchases worth a full ounce of gold are unlikely to be made, so smaller denominations take up even less space.

Bitcoin is indeed superior to precious metals when it comes to portability. It doesn't even have a physical footprint. You could keep trillions of dollars worth of assets on a piece of hardware that fits in the palm of your hand.

Moving gold worth one billion dollars (currently more than 20 tons) requires enormous effort and cost. Even with cash, you should be carrying several pallets full of $100 bills. With Bitcoin, you can send the same amount anywhere in the world for less than a dollar.

Divisibility

Another vital quality of money is its divisibility - that is, the ability to divide it into smaller units. With gold, you can take a one-ounce coin and cut it in half to make two half-ounce units. You may spoil the beautiful eagle or buffalo design on it, but the value of the gold remains the same. You can cut half-ounce units over and over to produce even smaller denominations.

Divisibility is another area where Bitcoin excels. There are only twenty-one million coins, but each is made up of one hundred million smaller units (satoshi). This gives users a high degree of control over their transactions, as they can send an amount by specifying up to eight decimal places. Additionally, Bitcoin's visibility makes it easier for small investors to buy fractions of BTC.

Reserve of value, medium of exchange and unit of account

The general opinion is divided on the current role of Bitcoin. Many believe that Bitcoin is simply a currency - a tool for moving funds from point A to point B. We will discuss this in the next section, but this perspective goes against what many proponents of the store of value thesis advocate.

Store of value proponents argue that Bitcoin has to go through various stages before becoming the definitive currency. It starts as a collector's item (probably the stage we are in now): it has proven functional and safe, but has only been adopted by a small niche. Its main audience consists of enthusiasts and speculators. Only with better education, infrastructure for institutions and greater confidence in its ability to retain value can it proceed to the next stage: the store of value. Some believe it has already reached this level, since institutions are investing in Bitcoin as well.

At this point, Bitcoin has not been widely spent due to Gresham's law, which states that bad money drives out good. This means that when presented with two types of coins, individuals will be prompted to spend the lower one and accumulate the higher one. Bitcoin users prefer to spend fiat currencies, as they have little confidence in their long-term survival. They prefer to keep their own bitcoins, as they believe they will hold their value.

If the Bitcoin network continues to grow, more and more users will adopt it, liquidity will increase, and the price will become more stable. Due to the increased stability, there will no longer be an incentive to keep it in the hope of big gains in the future. Hence, we can expect that it will be used a lot more in daily trading and payments, as a strong medium of exchange.

The increased use further stabilizes the price. In the final stage, Bitcoin would become a unit of account - it would be used to price other assets. Just as we could price a gallon of oil at $4, in a world where Bitcoin reigns as a currency we are going to measure this value in bitcoin.

If these three monetary milestones are met, proponents see a future where Bitcoin has become a new standard that replaces the currencies used today.

The case against Bitcoin as a store of value

The arguments presented in the previous pages may seem completely logical to some or completely absurd to others. There are some criticisms of the idea of Bitcoin as "digital gold" put forward by both Bitcoin enthusiasts and cryptocurrency skeptics.

Bitcoin as digital money

When disagreement arises on this issue, many are quick to point out the Bitcoin whitepaper. For them, it is clear that from the very beginning Satoshi designed Bitcoin to be spent. In fact, we find it in the same title of the document: “Bitcoin: A Peer-to-Peer Electronic Money System”.

The argument suggests that Bitcoin can only be valid if users spend their coins. By accumulating them, you are not helping adoption - you are hindering it. While Bitcoin is not widely valued as digital money, its core proposition is driven not by utility but by speculation.

In 2017, these ideological differences led to a major fork. Bitcoiner's minority wanted a system with larger blocks, to offer lower transaction fees. Due to the growth in usage of the original network, the cost of a transaction can drastically increase, excluding lower value transactions for many users. If the average commission is $10, there is little point in spending coins on a $3 purchase.

The forked network is now known as Bitcoin Cash. The original network implemented an update around that time, known as SegWit. Segwit nominally increased the capacity of the blocks, but that was not his main goal. It also laid the foundation for the Lightning Network, which aims to facilitate low-cost transactions by moving them off-chain.

However, the Lightning Network is far from perfect. Regular Bitcoin transactions are much easier to understand, while managing Lightning Network capacity and channels has a steep learning curve. It remains to be seen whether it can be simplified, or whether the solution design is fundamentally too complex to rationalize.

Due to the growing demand for block space, on-chain transactions are no longer very cheap during busy times. For this, it could be argued that not increasing the block size damages Bitcoin's functionality as a currency.

No intrinsic value

For many, the comparison between gold and Bitcoin is absurd. The history of gold is, essentially, the history of civilization. Precious metal has been a staple of societies for thousands of years. Undoubtedly, it has lost some of its dominance since the elimination of the gold standard, but it remains the ultimate safe haven asset.

Indeed, the comparison between the network effects of the king of assets and a protocol that has been in existence for eleven years seems a bit too much. Gold has been revered for millennia as both a status symbol and an industrial metal.

Conversely, Bitcoin has no use outside its network. You can't use it as a conductor in electronics, nor can you work it to create a huge shiny chain when you decide to become a hip hop star. It might emulate gold (mining, limited supply, etc.), but that doesn't change the fact that it's a digital asset. In a sense, all currencies are a shared belief - the dollar only has value because the government says it and society accepts it. Gold is only valuable because everyone agrees it does. Bitcoin is no different at all, but those who value it are still a small group in the overall world of finance.

Volatility and correlation to other assets

Those who discovered Bitcoin in the early years have certainly seen their investment grow by huge orders of magnitude. For them, it has actually retained value - and more. However, those who first bought coins near the all-time high did not have this experience. Many have suffered large losses by selling at any later time.

Bitcoin is incredibly volatile, and its markets are unpredictable. Metals like gold and silver have insignificant fluctuations by comparison. You may argue that we are still in the early stages, and that the price will eventually stabilize. But this, in itself, would indicate that Bitcoin is not currently a store of value.

The relationship between Bitcoin and traditional markets must also be considered. Since the launch of Bitcoin, they have been in a constant uptrend.

Cryptocurrency cannot truly be tested as a safe haven asset if all other asset classes are doing well as well. Bitcoin enthusiasts may refer to it as "unrelated" to other assets, but there is no way to know until other assets suffer while Bitcoin remains stable.

Tulipmania and Beanie Babies

It wouldn't be a real critique of Bitcoin's store-of-value properties if we didn't mention the comparisons to Tulipmania and the Beanie Babies. They are weak analogies at best, but they serve to illustrate the dangers of bubbles and their bursting.

In both episodes, investors flocked to buy items they thought were rare in hopes of reselling them for a profit. By themselves, the items weren't that valuable - they were relatively simple to produce. The bubble burst when investors realized they were massively overvaluing their investments, and as a result the tulip and beanie babies markets collapsed.

Again, these are weak analogies. Bitcoin's value comes from users' trust in it, but unlike tulips it cannot be grown to meet demand. That said, there is no guarantee that investors won't see Bitcoin as overvalued in the future, causing the bubble to burst.

Bitcoin certainly shares most of the characteristics of a store of value like gold. The number of units is limited, the network is decentralized enough to offer security to owners, and can be used to store and transfer value.

Ultimately, it has yet to prove itself as a safe haven - it is still too early to be certain. Things could go either way - the world could take refuge in Bitcoin in times of economic crisis, or it could continue to be used only by a minority group.

Only time will tell, but what we have seen since March 2020 is a progressive shift from bonds, gold and silver to Bitcoin and cryptocurrencies. We strongly believe Bitcoin is a store of value and we are dollar cost averaging into it on a weekly basis.

Chapter 19

Bitcoin Scams and How to Avoid Them

The blockchain industry has several cryptocurrency-related scams. Some of the most common include blackmail, fake exchanges, fake giveaways, social media phishing, copy-paste malware, phishing emails, Ponzi and pyramid schemes, and ransomware. In this chapter we are going to analyze some of these scams, so that you have the knowledge not to fall for them. In fact, when it comes to Bitcoin and cryptocurrency, the most important thing is being able to protect your assets. We are sure the next few pages are going to be extremely important.

Until new technologies are introduced to the world, scammers will continue to search for new tricks to deceive victims. Sadly, Bitcoin gives scammers in the crypto industry an interesting opportunity by being a borderless digital currency.

The decentralized nature of Bitcoin allows you to be in full control of your tokens. However, it also makes it more difficult to design an adequate regulatory and legal framework, as we have seen in a previous chapter. If scammers manage to convince you to make mistakes while using Bitcoin, they could steal your BTC, and there is practically nothing you can do to get back your coins.

That said, it is vital that you understand how scammers operate and find out how to identify potential red flags. There are a ton of scams involving Bitcoin to keep an eye out for. In this chapter we discuss the most common ones.

Blackmail

Blackmail is a method used by many scammers to threaten victims with the disclosure of sensitive information unless rewarded in some way. This reward typically comes in the form of a cryptocurrency payment.
In this scam, criminals obtain sensitive information about the victim and exploit it to force them to send Bitcoin or other forms of money.

The best way to avoid blackmail and protect your bitcoins is to be very careful when selecting your login credentials, which sites you visit online and who you give your information to. Also, using two-factor authentication whenever possible is another great help. If the information you are being blackmailed with is false and you find it out before sending the payment, you may be out of trouble.

Fake exchanges

As the name suggests, fake exchanges are fraudulent copies of legitimate crypto exchanges. Typically, these scams present themselves as mobile apps, but you may also find them in the form of desktop apps or fake websites. Some fake exchanges are very similar to the original versions, so you need to be very careful. They may seem legitimate at first glance, but their goal is to steal your money.

Typically, these fake exchanges attract crypto traders and investors by offering them free cryptocurrencies, competitive prices, minimal fees, and even gifts. To avoid getting scammed on a fake exchange, you should save the real URL as a bookmark in your browser and always double check before logging in. You can also use Binance Verify, a tool that allows you to verify the legitimacy of URLs, Telegram groups, Twitter accounts, and more.

For mobile apps, check out the developer's information, number of downloads, reviews and comments.

Fake giveaways

Fake giveaways are used to steal cryptocurrencies by offering something for free in exchange for a small deposit. Typically, scammers will ask you to first send funds to a Bitcoin address in order to receive more bitcoins in return (e.g., "send 0.1 BTC to receive 0.5 BTC"). However, if you make these transactions, you will not receive anything and you will never see your funds again.

There are many variations of scams involving fake giveaways. Instead of BTC, some scams will ask for other cryptocurrencies, such as ETH, BNB, XRP and many others. In some cases, they may ask for your private keys or other sensitive information.

Fake giveaways are usually found on Twitter and other social media platforms, where scammers latch onto popular tweets, viral news, or announcements (like a protocol update or an upcoming ICO).

The best way to avoid this type of scam is to never participate in any kind of giveaway that requires you to submit something of value first. Legitimate giveaways will never ask for funds.

Social media phishing

Social media phishing is a common Bitcoin scam that, like fake giveaways, it is often found on social media platforms. First of all, the scammers create an account that resembles that of someone with a high level of authority in the crypto industry. After that, they will offer fake giveaways via tweets or direct messages.

The best way to protect yourself from social media phishing is to verify that the person is really who they say they are. Some platforms have indicators to find out, such as checking verified accounts on Twitter and Facebook.

Copy-paste malware

Copy-paste malware is a very stealthy method used by scammers to steal your funds. This type of malware tampers with data on your device and, if you are not careful, it tricks you into sending money directly to the scammers.

Let's say you want to send a payment in BTC to your friend Bob. As usual, he sends you his Bitcoin address so you can copy and paste it into your wallet. However, if your device is infected with copy-paste malware, the scammer's address will automatically replace Bob's address the moment you paste it. This means that as soon as your Bitcoin transaction is sent and confirmed, you will have paid the scammer and Bob will not receive the coins.

To avoid this type of scam, you need to pay close attention to the security of your computer. Be wary of suspicious messages or emails that contain infected attachments or dangerous links. Pay attention to the websites you visit and the software you install on your devices. You should also consider using an antivirus and periodic scans for threats. Also, it's important to keep your device's operating system up-to-date and manually check the address before confirming the transaction.

Phishing emails

There are different types of phishing. One of the most common involves phishing emails that try to trick you into downloading an infected file or clicking a link that leads to an apparently legitimate malicious website. These emails are especially dangerous when they simulate a product or service you use frequently.

Typically, scammers include a message urging you to take urgent action to protect your account or funds. They may ask you to update your account information, reset your password or submit documents. In most cases, their goal is to get your login credentials and try to hack your account.

The first step in protecting yourself from phishing is to check if the emails are from the original source. If in doubt, you can contact the company directly to confirm that the email received was sent by them. Additionally, you can move your mouse over the email links (without clicking) to check if the URLs have misspellings, unusual characters, or other irregularities.

Even if you don't find any warning signs, you should avoid clicking on these links. If you need to log into your account, do it in another way, such as manually typing the URL or using your saved bookmarks.

Ponzi and pyramid schemes

Ponzi and pyramid schemes are two of the oldest financial scams. A Ponzi scheme is an investment strategy that distributes returns to long-time engaged investors using the funds added by new investors. When the scammer can no longer introduce new investors, the money stops flowing. OneCoin is a good example of a Ponzi scheme in crypto.

A pyramid scheme is a business model that pays members based on the number of new members they introduce. When the new members run out, the money runs out.

The best way to avoid these scams is to research cryptocurrencies before buying them - be it an altcoin or Bitcoin. If the value of a cryptocurrency or a Bitcoin fund is solely dependent on the enrollment of new investors or members, it is likely a Ponzi or pyramid scheme.

Ransomware

Ransomware is a type of malware that blocks victims' mobile devices or computers or prevents them from accessing important data - unless a ransom is paid (usually in BTC). These attacks can be particularly destructive when they target hospitals, airports and government agencies.
Typically, the ransomware will block access to important files or databases and threaten to delete them if payment is not made within the deadline. Unfortunately, however, there are no guarantees that the criminals will honor their promise.

There are some measures that allow you to protect yourself from ransomware attacks. The best practices are the following.

- Install an antivirus and keep your operating system and applications up to date.
- Do not click on suspicious advertisements and links.
- Pay attention to email attachments. You should be especially wary of .exe, .vbs or .scr files).
- Backup your files regularly to restore them in case of an attack.

As you might have noticed, the world of Bitcoin could be extremely dangerous if you do not put in place the right protective measures. However, if you are careful and have the right knowledge, it is also the most secure method to store your wealth. Please, dedicate some time to the study of this topic, as it as important as deciding your investing strategy.

Chapter 20

Bitcoin Update: the Lightning Network

In this chapter we are going to discuss a very interesting topic, that forever changed the history of the Bitcoin network when it was implemented. We are talking about the Lightning Network. Let's take a closer look at what it is.

The Lightning Network concept was created by Joseph Poon and Thaddeus Dryja in 2015. The main idea behind the project is the development of a payment protocol that can be used as an off-chain solution to address the problem of the scalability that plagues the Bitcoin blockchain, although the concept is also applicable to other cryptocurrencies.

The introduction of the Lightning Network is the answer to the limitations that both Bitcoin and many other cryptocurrencies face. Currently, the Bitcoin blockchain is capable of processing 2 to 7 transactions per second. With the growth of the cryptocurrency ecosystem and with more and more people joining the network, transactions transmitted to the blockchain are likely to increase. Gradually, the network becomes more and more congested and the overall performance is compromised, significantly reducing the practical usability of Bitcoin as a global digital currency. In this context, the Lightning Network was created as an attempt to reduce the congestion of the Bitcoin blockchain network.

How the Lightning Network works

The Lightning Network is composed of an off-chain transfer network developed on the Bitcoin blockchain. The system operates at a peer-to-peer (P2P) level and its use is based on the creation of so-called "two-way payment channels", through which users can perform direct cryptocurrency transactions.

When two counterparties decide to open a payment channel, they have the ability to transfer funds from one wallet to another. Even though the process of creating a new payment channel involves an on-chain transaction, all transactions that take place within the channel are off-chain and do not require global consent. As a result, these transactions can be quickly executed through a smart contract, incurring significantly lower fees and a significantly higher TPS (transactions per second) rate.

To open a payment channel, the two interested counterparties must set up a multi-signature wallet and add funds to it. The funds within the multi-signature wallet are accessible only when the private keys of both parties are provided (two or more, depending on the case). This means that one of the parties cannot access the wallet without the consent of the other.

As an example, suppose Alice wants to use the Lightning Network to trade bitcoins with Bob. First of all, the two open a payment channel, using a multi-signature wallet. While the payment channel works like a smart contract, the multi-signature wallet acts as a safe, where the funds to be exchanged are deposited. As long as the payment channel remains open, Alice and Bob can perform as many off-chain transactions as they want.

Immediately after each transaction, both Alice and Bob sign and update their copy of the balance sheet, which records the number of coins in their possession. When they no longer need it, they can close the payment channel and transmit the final balance to the Bitcoin blockchain. The Lightning Network smart contract guarantees that both parties will receive their bitcoins, based on the final version of the financial statements.

In other words, participants only need to interact with the Bitcoin blockchain twice. One to open the payment channel and one to close it. As a result, all transactions performed within the channel do not interact directly with the main chain.

Network Routing

Even if two counterparties do not have a direct payment channel available, they can still send and receive bitcoins through interconnected payment channels. This means that Alice can send funds to Charlie without having to create a direct channel with him, as long as there is a route between them that contains sufficient funds.

Therefore, if Alice has an open payment channel with Bob and Bob has a channel with Charlie, Alice can send bitcoins through Bob. Payment routing may involve several nodes of the Lightning Network, but the smart contract will automatically search for the shortest path available.

Benefits of the Lightning Network

As we have seen, the Lightning Network project is working to achieve an off-chain solution that solves the scalability problem. If successful, it could reduce traffic on the Bitcoin blockchain. Through the use of

two-way payment channels, the Lightning Network makes almost instant transactions possible.
The Lightning Network could prove suitable for micropayments, as it allows the transfer of very small amounts, even reaching 1 satoshi. In addition, the machine-to-machine economy could implement automated micropayments, in which transactions are performed between electronic devices without the need for human intervention.

Limits of the Lightning Network

Unlike on-chain transactions, within the Lightning Network it is not possible to make payments if the recipient is offline. Therefore, the network participants may need to monitor payment channels regularly to protect their funds (this risk can be eliminated by using external monitoring services).
Furthermore, the Lightning Networkis not suitable for large payments. The network is based on several multi-signature wallets (in practice shared wallets), and it is very likely that these do not contain a sufficient balance to act as intermediaries for large

payments. Opening and closing a payment channel requires an on-chain transaction, which usually requires labor and higher fees.

When will the Lightning Network be implemented?

Taking into consideration the beta version of the mainnet announced by Lightning Labs, the launch date of the Lightning Network had been set for March 15th, 2018. However, the Lightning Network has not yet been actually implemented on the Bitcoin blockchain.

Following the launch of the beta, there has been a huge increase in the number of Lightning Network nodes and payment channels. Some exchanges, like Kraken, announced that they will start supporting the Lightning Network in 2021.

The collective work of nodes and payment channels is what makes Lightning Network an interesting solution to the problem of scalability. The beta version is currently being tested and its efficiency is yet to be proven. Despite this, the Lightning Network has enormous potential to improve the Bitcoin and cryptocurrency ecosystem.

The Lightning Torch

On January 19, 2019, pseudonymous Twitter user “hodlonaut” began a game-like promotional test of the Lightning Network by sending 100,000 satoshis (0.001 bitcoin) to a trusted recipient where each recipient added 10,000 satoshis to send to the next trusted recipient. The so-called "lightning torch" payment reached notable personalities. Among them there were Lightning Labs CEO Elizabeth Stark, Twitter CEO Jack Dorsey, and Binance CEO "CZ" Changpeng Zhao. The lightning torch was passed 292 times before reaching the formerly hard-coded limit of 4,390,000 satoshis. The final payment of the lightning torch was sent on April 13th, 2019 as a donation of 4,290,000 satoshis ($217.78 at the time) to Bitcoin Venezuela, a non-profit association that promotes bitcoin in Venezuela. We had the privilege to participate in the Lightning Torch and we are extremely proud of that event.

Chapter 21

The SegWit Update

Segregated Witness (SegWit) is an update to the protocol developed in 2015. The concept was introduced as a solution to the scalability problem that blockchain networks still face today.

On average, the Bitcoin network validates a new block every 10 minutes, each containing several transactions. Consequently, the size of the block affects the number of transactions that can be confirmed in each block. Currently, the Bitcoin blockchain is capable of processing around 7 transactions per second.

The core idea of SegWit is to reorganize the block data so that the signatures are no longer placed along with the transaction data. In other words, the SegWit update consists of separating witnesses (signatures) from transaction data. This allows multiple transactions to be stored in a single block, thus increasing the performance in terms of transactions on the network.

Considering that Bitcoin can process around 7 transactions per second, executing a transaction can sometimes take a long time. This process is far slower than conventional payment solutions and financial networks, which can process thousands of transactions per second.

SegWit was developed in 2015 by Bitcoin developer Pieter Wuille, along with other Bitcoin Core contributors. In August 2017, the SegWit update was implemented as a soft fork on the Bitcoin network.
There are several cryptocurrency projects using SegWit today, including Bitcoin and Litecoin. The protocol update brought with it a number of benefits, including improved transaction speed and increased block capacity. Additionally, SegWit has fixed the so-called transaction malleability bug (more on that later).

Increase in block capacity

One of the biggest advantages of SegWit is the increase in block capacity. By removing signature data from transaction input, more transactions can be stored in a single block.

Transactions are made up of two main components: inputs and outputs. Essentially, an input contains the public address of the sender, while the output contains the public address of the recipient. However, the sender must prove ownership of the funds they are transferring, and they do so with a digital signature. Without SegWit, signature data can take up to 65% of a block. With SegWit, the signature data is removed from the transaction input. This brings the actual block size from 1MB to approximately 4MB.

It is important to note that SegWit is not an actual block size increase. Instead, it is an advanced solution that allows you to increase the actual size without having to increase the block size limit (which would require a hard fork). To be more precise, the current block size is still 1MB, but the actual block size limit is 4MB.

SegWit also introduced the idea of block weight. We can consider the weight of the block as a concept that replaces the idea of block size. Essentially, the block weight is a measure that includes all data in the block, including transaction data (1MB) and signature data (3MB), which are no longer part of the input field.

Increased transaction speed

By creating a block that can hold more transactions, SegWit has also made it possible to increase transaction speed, as there can be a larger number of transactions moving through the blockchain. While a block may take the same time to mine, more transactions are being processed in it, so the transactions per second rate is higher.

The increase in transaction speed has also helped reduce transaction costs in the Bitcoin network. Before SegWit, it wasn't uncommon to spend more than $30 on a transaction. However, SegWit has drastically lowered this cost to less than $ 1 per transaction.

Correction of transaction malleability

In the past, a major problem with Bitcoin was the ability to potentially alter transaction signatures. If a signature is altered, it could result in the corruption of a transaction between two parties. Since the data stored on blockchains is virtually immutable, it would have been possible to permanently store invalid transactions on the blockchain.

With SegWit, signatures are no longer part of the transaction data, which removes the possibility of altering this data. This fix has enabled further innovations in the blockchain community, including second-layer protocols and smart contracts.

SegWit and Lightning Network

The development of second-layer protocols was partially made possible by the correction of the transaction malleability bug. In a nutshell, second-layer protocols are new platforms or new products developed on top of a blockchain, such as that of Bitcoin. As we have seen in the last chapter, one of the best known second-layer protocols is Lightning Network, an off-chain micropayment network.

SegWit vs SegWit2x

SegWit is a soft fork upgrade, which means it is backwards compatible. In other words, Bitcoin nodes that are not updated to include SegWit are still capable of processing transactions. However, another SegWit implementation called SegWit2x (S2X) has been proposed, which would have required a hard fork upgrade.

The key difference between SegWit and SegWit2x is that the latter would not only involve a change in transaction batching, but also an increase in block size (from 1MB to 2MB). However, a larger block size would have increased the load on node operators and miners, as it would have led to double the amount of data to manage.

Another important difference is that the SegWit proposal was supported and enforced by the Bitcoin community. The episode gave birth to the concept of UASF, which stands for user-activated soft fork.

Conversely, SegWit2x proposed a substantial change to one of Bitcoin's core rules, and as the developers did not reach a consensus on its adoption and implementation, the SegWit2x movement was suspended.
SegWit's implementation marked the biggest update to the Bitcoin protocol, and the fact that it has been supported and implemented by the decentralized community makes it even more important.

The introduction of SegWit was a major step forward in solving many problems related to Bitcoin and other blockchain networks - especially in terms of scalability. Through the combination of SegWit and second-layer protocols, blockchain networks can handle more transactions, with more efficiency and lower costs.

Despite being a powerful and innovative solution, SegWit has not yet reached full adoption. Currently, the percentage of Bitcoin addresses using SegWit is around 53%.

Chapter 22

Schnorr Signatures

As you may know, Bitcoin enforces property rights through what we call the Elliptic Curve Digital Signature Algorithm (or ECDSA). The algorithm allows you to take a number (i.e., a private key) and derive a public key from it.

The magic of this step is that while it is simple for you to get the public key from the private key, the reverse is impossible. Your private key is your passport to the Bitcoin network. It is what allows you to generate an address to receive coins and spend them later.

In this chapter, we will talk about the Schnorr signature algorithm, an alternative to ECDSA that could introduce some interesting changes in Bitcoin.

A summary on digital signatures

Digital signatures work just like their ancestors on pen and paper, but they are much more secure. With a little time and effort, anyone can forge a signature on paper. You can't do the same with a solid digital signature scheme, even with hundreds of thousands of years at your disposal.

There are several use cases for digital signatures. One of the most popular involves proving to the world that you wrote a particular message. As mentioned, you can create a public key from a private key. To do this, just perform some mathematical fantasy on the secp256k1 curve. After that, you can also generate a public address from your public key. Wait, you don’t know what the secp256k1 curve is? Do not worry, if you are just starting out studying Bitcoin, it is not something worth explaining as it has more to do with cryptography than cryptocurrencies.

You just need to know that it is completely safe to show your public key to anyone. You can add it to your website or Twitter bio to allow others to verify your identity. Likewise, you can share your public addresses with others to transfer cryptocurrencies.

Your private key allows you to create a digital signature. By writing a message and performing an operation on it using your private key, you create a signed message. Anyone can review it and compare it to your public key to verify that it was indeed signed by you.

How does this relate to Bitcoin? Whenever you make a transaction in Bitcoin, you are digitally signing a message that says "I am sending these coins which have previously been sent to me". Then, when it is sent to the other nodes on the network, they can check that the ECDSA signature matches the message. If not, the nodes reject it.

What are Schnorr's signatures?

Schnorr signatures are a different type of algorithm. It operates similar to the Elliptic Curve Digital Signature Algorithm we currently use, but has a number of advantages over it. Schnorr's signatures are actually older than the ECDSA, which leads many to wonder why they haven't been integrated into Bitcoin from the start.

One possible explanation is that Claus P. Schnorr - the creator of the algorithm - patented them. The patents expired in early 2008, months before the publication of the Bitcoin whitepaper, but the algorithm still lacked general standardization. For this reason, Satoshi Nakamoto has opted for the more widely accepted (and open source) ECDSA.

Benefits of Schnorr signatures

Schnorr's signatures are quite simple in comparison to other algorithms. As a result, they are safer than their alternatives. It might not mean much at first glance, but they have another powerful feature: linearity.

Simply put, this makes the algorithm particularly attractive for certain businesses - in particular, for multi-signature transactions. You may know that

Bitcoin already supports multi sigs, but not in the best way.

When you create a multisignature address, anyone who sends you funds does not need to know what conditions you have set for spending inputs. They may not even know they are sending funds to a multisig setup. In fact, the only noticeable difference of the address is the fact that it starts with a "3".

However, you reveal its nature when you want to move funds. Let's assume you used a 2-of-3 setup with Alice and Bob. To spend 5 BTC, all three of you must provide public keys and valid signatures. When you move the funds out of the address, the entire network can know what happened by examining the blockchain.

From a privacy standpoint, that's not good news. Also, if you create a larger multisig (e.g., 8-of-10), you are taking up a lot of space on the blockchain. This can be expensive, as it will result in a longer transaction - remember that the more bytes there are in your transaction, the more you will have to pay to get it through the network.

Schnorr's signatures were presented as a solution to these privacy and scalability issues. They allow things like signature aggregation, which combines the signatures of several signers into a single signature. The resulting “master signature” will be the same length as a normal individual signature, leading to significant space savings.

Additionally, combined signatures make it much more difficult for an observer to determine who signed a transaction. In m-of-m schemes (where all participants have to sign in to spend the funds), you wouldn't even be able to distinguish between single and multisig transactions.

Essentially, Schnorr's signatures are an important component for further progress. Once implemented, they can be leveraged to improve crypto technologies such as atomic swaps and the Lightning Network.

The implementation of Schnorr signatures

As with most updates to the Bitcoin protocol, it may take some time for the general community of Bitcoin users to agree to include Schnorr's signatures. Bitcoin Core contributors Pieter Wuille, Jonas Nick, and Tim Ruffing have submitted a draft of the Bitcoin Improvement Proposal (BIP), but there is still work to be done.

Blockstream has already released one possible implementation called MuSig. By allowing signature and key aggregation, it could form the basis for the Bitcoin's Schnorr signature algorithm.

Schnorr's signatures could be integrated into the code through a soft fork, which is a change that would not divide the network. This type of fork would be an "opt-in" update. However, it would be too optimistic to assume that we will see them integrated in the near future - it may take a couple of years before consensus is reached.

Schnorr's signatures are one of the most anticipated targets on Bitcoin's current roadmap. With a single update, they can provide significant privacy and scalability benefits. Perhaps more interestingly, they also create the conditions for further developments in Bitcoin smart contracts and more advanced constructs such as Taproot, which we will discuss in the next chapter.

Chapter 23

Taproot

Along with Schnorr's signatures, Taproot is a highly anticipated Bitcoin tech upgrade since the introduction of SegWit. Taproot's goal is to change the way Bitcoin scripts operate to improve privacy, scalability and security. This and much more will be possible by combining Taproot with a related update, Schnorr's signatures.

Anyone familiar with the crypto community knows that privacy, scalability and security are top priorities. Even though Bitcoin is the most popular cryptocurrency in the world, those issues still need to be addressed. Taproot aims to do exactly that.

Bitcoin has had its ups and downs, but it has proven to be the pillar holding the crypto universe in place. Regardless of incidents over the years, such as the hack against Mt.Gox or the famous Bitcoin hard forks, the crypto community has continued to support Bitcoin.

However, there are certain issues that cannot be ignored and one of the biggest is privacy. Bitcoin is a public blockchain, anyone can monitor the transactions that take place on the network. For some people, this is a major problem.

You can increase your anonymity through techniques such as coin mixing and CoinJoins. Unfortunately, none of these make Bitcoin a private currency. While the same goes for Taproot, it could help increase anonymity on the network. The Taproot update is considered by many to be an important first step in resolving Bitcoin's lack of privacy and other related issues. But what exactly is Taproot, and how will it benefit Bitcoin? Let's find it out together.

What is Taproot?

Taproot is a soft fork that improves Bitcoin scripts to increase privacy and other factors related to complex transactions. Transactions on the Bitcoin network can use various features that make them more complex, including timed issues, multi-signature requirements, and more.

Without Taproot, anyone can identify transactions that use these complex features, which require the creation of multiple transactions. However, the Taproot update will allow you to "hide" all the moving parts of a Bitcoin transaction that includes such complexities. Therefore, even if the transactions adopt these functions, they will appear as a single transaction. This is a big win for Bitcoin privacy advocates.

In fact, Taproot allows you to completely hide the execution of a Bitcoin script. For example, spending Bitcoin using Taproot can make a transaction in a Lightning Network channel, a peer-to-peer transaction, or a sophisticated smart contract indistinguishable. However, it should be noted that this does not change the fact that the wallets of the initial sender and the final recipient will be exposed.

The Taproot proposal was initially presented by Greg Maxwell, developer of Bitcoin Core, in January 2018. In October 2020, Taproot was integrated into the Bitcoin Core library after a pull request from Pieter Wuille. To fully implement the update, node operators must adopt Taproot's new consensus rules. Depending on this dynamic, the actual implementation could take months.

The benefits of Taproot for Bitcoin

As we have already mentioned, Taproot will bring major improvements to Bitcoin's privacy. Combined with Schnorr's signatures, Taproot could also increase the efficiency in executing transactions. In addition to increased privacy, other potential benefits include the following.

- Reduced amount of data to be transferred and stored in the blockchain;

- More transactions per block (higher transactions per second rate);
- Reduced transaction costs.

Another advantage of Taproot is the fact that signatures will no longer be malleable, a known security risk in the Bitcoin network. Simply put, the malleability of signatures means that it is technically possible to change the signature of a transaction before it is confirmed. By doing so, the attack would make it appear that the transaction never took place. This leaves Bitcoin vulnerable to the notorious double spend problem, which could ruin the integrity of the distributed ledger.

As you may understand by now, Taproot is a highly anticipated and widely supported upgrade to Bitcoin. When implemented alongside Schnorr's signatures, we will see dramatic improvements in privacy, scalability, and security. Additionally, these updates can generate increased interest in the Lightning Network and encourage multi-signature solutions as the industry standard.

Regardless of the level of your involvement in the Bitcoin community, the benefits of improving privacy, efficiency and security will likely affect your experience when using Bitcoin. We could not be more excited for this incredible update!

Chapter 24

Bitcoin and the Evolution of the Web

The internet has changed dramatically since its creation. From Internet Relay Chat (IRC) to modern social media, it has become a vital part of human interactions - and continues to evolve.

Web 3.0 is the next generation of Internet technology, and it relies heavily on the use of machine learning and artificial intelligence (AI). Its goal is to create more open, connected and smarter websites and web applications that focus on automated data understanding.

Through the use of AI and advanced machine learning techniques, Web 3.0 aims to deliver more personalized and relevant information at a faster rate. This is possible thanks to the use of intelligent search algorithms and developments in Big Data analytics.

Current websites typically have static information or user-posted content, such as forums and social media. While this allows information to be distributed to a large group of people, it may not meet the needs of a specific user. A website should be able to personalize the information it offers to each individual user, similar to the dynamics that characterizes human communication in the real world.

In Web 3.0, an ocean of information will be available to websites and web applications, which will be able to understand and use data in a way that is relevant to the individual user.

A brief history of the evolution of the Internet

Websites and web applications have changed dramatically over the past few decades. They have evolved from static sites to data-driven sites that users can interact with and modify.

Web 1.0

The original internet was based on what is now known as Web 1.0. The term was coined in 1999 by the author and web designer Darci DiNucci, to distinguish between Web 1.0 and Web 2.0. In the early 1990s, websites were being developed using static HTML pages that could only display information - there was no way for users to modify the data.

Web 2.0

That all changed in the late 1990s as the transition to a more interactive Internet began to take shape. With Web 2.0, users could interact with websites through the use of databases, server-side processing, forms and social media.

This has led to the transition from a static web to a more dynamic one. Web 2.0 has brought with it a greater emphasis on user-generated content and interoperability between different sites and applications. Web 2.0 was less observation and more participation. By the mid-2000s, most websites had made the transition to Web 2.0.

The future of the internet

Looking at the history of the Internet, the evolution of a more semantically intelligent web is logical. The data was initially presented statically to users. Later, users could interact with this data dynamically. Now all this data will be used by algorithms to improve the user experience and make the web more personalized and familiar.

Web 3.0, even if not yet fully defined, could exploit peer-to-peer (P2P) technologies such as blockchain, open-source software, virtual reality, Internet of Things (IoT) and much more. Currently, many applications are limited to running on a single operating system. Web 3.0 could enable applications by making them more device-agnostic, meaning they could operate on different types of hardware and software without any additional development costs.

Web 3.0 also aims to make the Internet more open and decentralized. In today's environment, users have to rely on network and telephony service providers to monitor the information passing through their systems. With the introduction of distributed ledger technologies, this could change very soon, and users could get their data back in their hands.

The advantages of Web 3.0

Web 3.0 offers huge advantages over its predecessors. Some of the benefits are the following.

- **No central points of control.** As middlemen are removed from the equation, user data is no longer under their control. This reduces the risk of censorship by governments or corporations and reduces the effectiveness of denial-of-service (DoS) attacks.

- **Greater interconnectivity of information**. As more products connect to the Internet, larger data sets give the algorithms more information to analyze. This can help them ensure more accurate information that meets the specific needs of the individual user.

- **More efficient navigation.** In the past, finding the best search engine result was quite challenging. However, over the years, these have improved in finding semantically relevant results based on the search context and metadata. This results in a more convenient web browsing experience that can help anyone find the exact information they need with relative ease.
  Web 2.0 has also introduced social tagging systems, which can be manipulated. With smarter algorithms, manipulated results can be filtered by AI.

- **Improved advertising and marketing**. Nobody likes to be bombarded with online advertisements. However, if the ads are relevant to the user's interests and needs, they can be useful instead of just being a waste of time. Web 3.0 aims to improve advertising by leveraging smarter AI systems and distinguishing specific audiences based on consumer data.

- **Best customer support**. When it comes to websites and web applications, customer service is key to a positive user experience. However, due to the enormous costs many successful web services fail to expand their customer service operations in a timely manner. Through the use of smarter chatbots that can speak to multiple customers at the same time, users can enjoy a superior experience when dealing with support agents.

The evolution of the internet has been a long journey and will certainly continue on to further iterations. With the enormous increase in data available, websites and web applications have the ability to move to a web that offers a significantly better experience to a growing number of users around the world.

While there is no concrete definition for Web 3.0 yet, it is already in place thanks to innovations in other technological fields and Bitcoin is certainly playing a role in this revolution, creating a smarter finance for everyone.

Chapter 25

Improving the Blockchain Scalability

In previous chapters we have mentioned the different updates that are being implemented on the Bitcoin blockchain to make it more scalable. In the next few pages we are going to dive deeper into this topic.

With the term scalability we refer to the skill of a system to grow to satisfy an increasing request. In computer technology, you could improve your device's performance by updating the hardware to make it faster in performing certain activities. When we talk about scalability in Blockchain, we refer to the growth of their ability to manage more transactions.

Protocols like Bitcoin have many strengths, but scalability is not one of these. If Bitcoin is managed in a centralized database, it would be relatively easy for an administrator to increase speed and performance. However, the value proposals of Bitcoin (e.g., resistance to censorship) require that many participants synchronize a copy of Blockchain.

Blockchain scalability problems

Performing a Bitcoin node is relatively cheap, and even simple devices can do it. Despite this, given that thousands of nodes must keep up to date with each other, there are some limits on their ability.

Limits are fixed on the number of transactions that can be processed on-chain, to prevent the database from being too heavy. If it became too big too quickly, the nodes could not keep up. Also, if the blocks are too large, it is not possible to send them quickly through the network.

As a result, we are faced with an obstacle. A blockchain can be seen as a train service that departs at defined intervals. Each wagon offers limited places, and to get a ticket. Travelers must make an offer to earn the place. If everyone tries to get on the train at the same time, the price will be high. Similarly, a clogged network with pending transactions will require users to pay higher commissions to ensure that their transactions are included in reasonable times.

A solution could be to enlarge the wagons. This would like to say more places, higher performance and lower prices for tickets. But there are no guarantees that places are not filled as in the previous case. The wagons cannot be enlarged constantly, as well as blocks on blocks and gases cannot expand to infinity. The latter makes it more expensive for nodes to stay on the network, as they need more advanced hardware to stay synchronized.

The creator of Ethereum, the second largest cryptocurrency, Vitalik Buterin coined the scalability trilemma to describe the challenge that blockchains must face. Butterin has theorized that protocols must compromise between scalability, safety and decentralization. These elements are in conflict between them. In fact, by concentrating too much on two of the properties, you will neglect the third one.

For this reason, many see scalability as something to reach off-chain, while security and decentralization should be maximized on the blockchain itself.

Off-chain scalability solutions

Off-chain scalability refers to approaches to perform transactions without weighing off the blockchain. Protocols that connect to the blockchain and allow users to send and receive funds, without transactions to appear on the main chain.

What is a sidechain?

A sidechain is a separate blockchain that is not an independent platform, as it is anchored in some way to the main chain. The main chain and the sidechain are interoperable, and the assets can flow freely from one to the other.

There are several ways to ensure that the funds can be transferred. In some cases, assets are moved from the main chain by depositing them into a special address. In fact, they are not actually sent to the sidechain - they are instead blocked in the address, and a corresponding amount is issued on the sidechain. A more linear option is to send funds to a custody service, which exchanges the deposit in funds on the sidechain. However, in this case centralization could become an issue.

The functionality of a sidechain

Suppose your friend Alice has five bitcoins. She wants to exchange them for five equivalent units on a Bitcoin sidechain - let's call it sidecoin. The sidechain in question uses a bidirectional anchorage, so users can transfer their own assets from the Main Chain to the Sidechain and vice versa.

Remember that the Sidechain is a separate blockchain. Therefore, it will have blocks, nodes and mechanisms

of different validation. To receive the sidecoin, Alice sends the five bitcoins to another address. It could be owned by someone who will credit the five sidecoin on her address once you received bitcoins. Alternatively, you could present some kind of trust-minimized configuration where the sidecoin are automatically credited when the software detects a payment.
Alice has now converted her coins into sidecoin, but she can always reverse the process to recover her bitcoins. Now that she has entered the sidechain, she is free to make transactions on this separate blockchain. She can send sidecoin or receive from others, just as it would happen on the main chain.

She might, for example, pay Bob a sidecoin for a logo. When she wants to go back to Bitcoin, she could send her four remaining sidecoin to a special address. Once the transaction is confirmed, four bitcoins would be unlocked and sent to an address that you control on the main chain.

Use cases of a sidechain

Maybe you're wondering what all this can serve. Why does not Alice directly use the Bitcoin blockchain?

The answer is that the sidechain could be capable of things that bitcoin is unable to do. Blockchain are accurately organized compromise systems. Although Bitcoin is the safest and most decentralized cryptocurrency, it is not the best in terms of performance. Bitcoin transactions are faster than conventional methods, but still relatively slow compared to other blockchain systems. The blocks are mined every ten minutes, and the commissions can grow greatly when the network is congested.

Indeed, it is likely that this level of security is not necessary for small daily payments. If Alice is paying a coffee, she will not wait for confirmation of the transaction. Her coffee would be cold before the payment is concluded.

The sidechain are not bound by the same rules. In fact, they don't even need to use the proof of work to

operate. You can use any consensus mechanism, trust a single validator, or change any parameter. You can introduce updates that do not exist on the main chain, produce larger blocks and impose quick regulations.
It is interesting to note that the sidechain could have critical bugs and it would not influence the underlying chain. This allows them to be used as a platform for experimentation and to implement functionality that would otherwise require consent from the majority of the network.

Provided that users are satisfied with compromises, sidechains could be a fundamental step towards effective scalability. The main chain nodes must not file every transaction from the sidechain. Alice could enter the sidechain with a single Bitcoin transaction, run hundreds of sidecoin transactions, and exit the sidechain. As for the Bitcoin Blockchain, she performed only two transactions - one to enter and one to go out.

Payment channels

Payment channels have the same purpose as the Sidechain on the scalability front, but are fundamentally very different. Like the sidechain, they push the transactions out of the main chain to prevent the blockchain from clogging. Unlike sidechain, however, they do not require a separate blockchain to work.

A payment channel uses a Smart Contract to allow users to perform transactions without publishing them on the blockchain. This is possible thanks to the use of an agreement imposed by software between the two participants.

How does a payment channel work?

In models like the famous Lightning Network, two parts first deposit the coins in an address they possess together. This is a multi-signature address, which requires two signatures to spend the funds. So, if Alice and Bob have created this address, the funds can only be moved with the consent of both.

Suppose they deposit 10 BTC each at an address that now contains 20 BTCs. It would be easy for them to keep a budget that begins by saying that Alice and Bob have 10 BTC each. If Alice wants to give Bob a coin, they could update the budget indicating that Alice has 9 BTC and Bob has 11 BTC. They should not publish the results on the Blockchain until they continue to update these budgets.

When they decide to end their transactions, they could create a transaction that sends these balances to the addresses in possession of the parts, sign it and transmit it.

Alice and Bob may have registered ten, one hundred or a thousand transactions on their budget. But as far as the blockchain is concerned, only two on-chain operations performed: one for the initial transaction and the other to realize the funds at the end. In addition to these two, all other transactions are free and almost instant. There are no costs to pay for miners and no confirmation of the block to wait.

Obviously, the example we discussed above requires the collaboration of both parties, a situation not ideal for two strangers. However, you can use special mechanisms to punish any fraud attempt, so that the parties can certainly interact without trusting each other.

Payment routing

Evidently the payment channels are convenient for two parts that provide a high volume of transactions. But it does not end here. It is possible to create a network of these channels to ensure that Alice can pay a participant to which it is not directly connected. If Bob has an open channel with Carol, Alice can pay her, as long as there is sufficient capacity. Alice will transmit the funds to the side of the Bob channel, which, in turn, will transmit them to that of Carol. If Carol is connected to another participant, she can do the same thing.

A network of this type evolves in a distributed typology in which anyone is connected to different peers. We will often find multiple paths to a destination, and users can choose the most effective one.
We discussed two scalability approaches that allow transactions to be carried out without weighing off the underlying blockchain. Both technologies, sidechain and payment channels, must still mature, but are already widely exploited by users who want to circumvent the deficiencies of transactions in the base level.

Over time and as other users join the network, it is important that decentralization remains intact. This is only possible through the imposition of limits on the growth of the blockchain to ensure that new nodes can easily join. Supporters of off-chain scalability solutions believe that, over time, the main chain will only be used to regulate high-value transactions, or to enter/exit Sidechain and open/close channels.

Chapter 26

The Stock to Flow Model

In this chapter we are going to take a look at a price prediction model called stock to flow. In simple terms, the Stock to Flow model (SF or S2F) is a way to measure the abundance of a particular resource. The Stock to Flow ratio is the quantity of resources present in the reserves divided by the quantity that is produced annually.

The Stock to Flow model is generally applied to natural resources. Let's take the example of gold. Although estimates may vary, the World Gold Council estimates that around 190,000 tons of gold have been mined in history. This quantity (that is, the total supply) is what we can call the stock. In addition,

approximately 2,500 to 3,200 tons of gold are mined each year. This quantity is what we call the flow.
We can calculate the Stock to Flow ratio using these two parameters.

But what does it mean in real life terms? Essentially it shows how many new units of a given resource enter the market each year, in relation to the total supply. The higher the Stock to Flow ratio, the less new supply enters the market relative to the total. Therefore, an asset with a high Stock to Flow ratio should, in theory, hold its value effectively over the long term.

Conversely, consumer goods and industrial products will generally have a low Stock to Flow ratio. For what reason? Since their value typically comes from their destruction or consumption, the stocks are usually only sufficient to cover the demand. These assets don't necessarily have a high value as possessions, so they tend to perform poorly as an investment asset. In some exceptional cases, the price could rise rapidly if a shortage is foreseen in the future. But other than that, production remains in step with demand.

It is important to emphasize that scarcity alone does not necessarily mean that a resource is precious. Gold, for example, is not that rare - after all, we have 190,000 tons available! The Stock to Flow report suggests that it is valuable because the annual production compared to the existing supply is relatively small and constant.

The Stock to Flow ratio of gold

Historically, gold has had the highest Stock to Flow ratio of all precious metals. But what is the exact number? Going back to our previous example - divide the total supply of 190,000 tons by 3,200, and you will get a Stock to Flow ratio of ~ 59. This tells us that, at the current rate of production, it would take around 59 years to mine 190,000 tons of gold.

However, it is worth bearing in mind that the estimates of the amount of new gold that will be mined each year are just that - estimates. If we increase the annual production (flow) to 3,500, the Stock to Flow ratio drops to ~ 54.

While we're at it, why not calculate the total value of all the gold that has been mined in history? If we take a price of around $ 1500 for every ounce of gold, the total value of all gold reaches around $9 trillion. That said it sounds like a lot, but if we combined all this gold into a cube we could make it fit on a single soccer field!

For comparison, the highest total value of the Bitcoin network hit $1 trillion at the beginning of 2021.

Stock to Flow and Bitcoin

By now you should know how Bitcoin works. Therefore, it won't be hard for you to understand why it might make sense to apply the Stock to Flow model to it. Essentially, this model treats bitcoins as limited resources, like gold or silver.

Gold and silver are often referred to as resources that act as a store of value. In theory, they should hold their long-term value due to their relative scarcity and low flow. Furthermore, it is somewhat difficult to significantly increase the supply in a short period of time.

According to supporters of the Stock to Flow model, Bitcoin is a similar asset. It is scarce, relatively expensive to produce, and its maximum supply is limited to 21 million coins. Furthermore, the issuance of supply of Bitcoin is defined at the protocol level, which makes the flow completely predictable. You should have already familiarized with the concept of halving, where the amount of new supply entering the system is halved every 210,000 blocks (roughly four years).

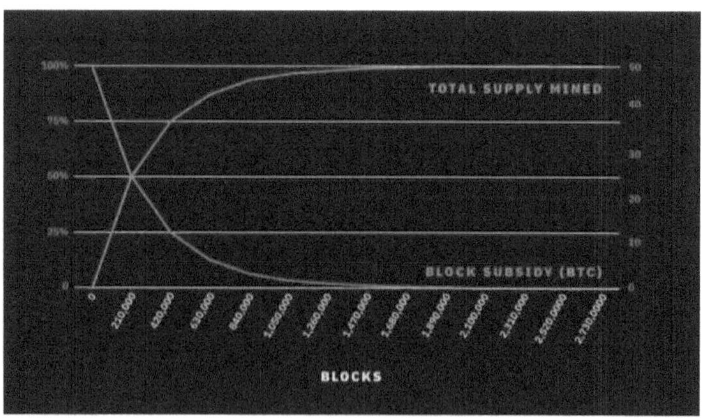

According to the proponents of this model, the combination of these properties creates a scarce digital asset with deeply valid characteristics for maintaining long-term value. Furthermore, they assume that there is a statistically significant relationship between the Stock to Flow and the market value. According to the model's projections, Bitcoin's price is expected to go through a noticeable increase over time due to its consistently low Stock to Flow ratio.

Among others, the application of the Stock to Flow model to Bitcoin is often attributed to PlanB and its article "Modeling Bitcoin's Value with Scarcity".

Bitcoin's Stock to Flow ratio

The current circulating supply of Bitcoin is around 18 million bitcoins, while the new supply is around 0.7 million per year. At the time of writing, Bitcoin's Stock to Flow ratio is hovering around 50.

In the image below, you can see the historical relationship between the 365-day moving average of Bitcoin's Stock to Flow and its price. We have also indicated the dates of the Bitcoin halving on the vertical axis.

Limits of the Stock to Flow model

While Stock to Flow is an interesting model for measuring scarcity, it doesn't explain all parts of the picture. The models depend entirely on their assumptions. First of all, Stock to Flow is based on the assumption that scarcity, as measured by the model, should bring value. According to critics of the Stock to Flow, this model fails if Bitcoin has no other useful quality besides supply shortages.

Gold's scarcity, predictable flow and global liquidity have made it a relatively stable store of value relative to fiat currencies, which are subject to devaluation. According to this model, Bitcoin's volatility is also expected to decrease over time. This is confirmed by historical data provided by Coinmetrics.

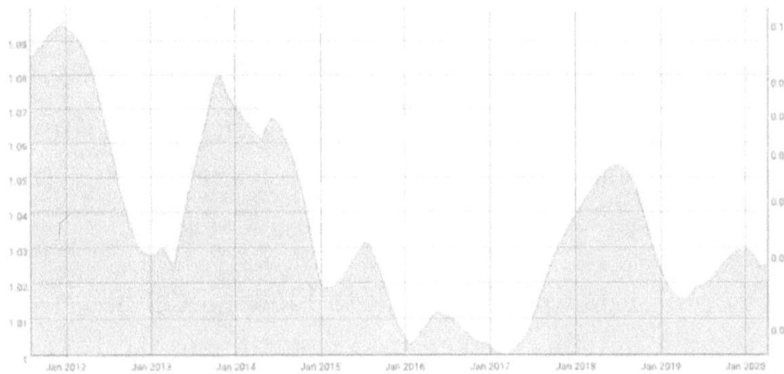

The valuation of an asset requires consideration of its volatility. If volatility is to some extent predictable, the valuation model may be more reliable. However, Bitcoin is famous for its large price swings.

While volatility may decrease at the macro level, Bitcoin has been valued in a free market since its inception. This means that the price is mostly self-adjusted on the free market by users, traders and speculators. Combining this with relatively low liquidity, Bitcoin is likely to be exposed to sudden spikes in volatility more than any other asset. Hence, the model may fail to consider this either.

Other external factors, such as economic Black Swan events, could undermine this model. However, it should be noted that this possibility essentially applies to any model that tries to predict the price of an asset based on historical data. A Black Swan event, by definition, has a surprise factor. Historical data cannot take into account unknown events.

Our opinion is that the Stock to Flow model has been incredibly accurate so far and that it will be able to predict future price movements for the foreseeable future.

Chapter 27

Revolutionizing the Banking System

Banks often act from intermediaries within the global economy by managing and coordinating the financial system through their internal registers. Given that these registers are not available to the public to be examined, people are forced to pay confidence in the banks and in their infrastructures often obsolete.

Blockchain technology has the potential to revolutionize not only the world's money market, but also the entire banking industry, eliminating these intermediaries and replacing them with a trustless, borderless, transparent and easy to access for everyone.

Blockchain could potentially help make the transactions fastest and most economical, increase access to capital, ensure greater data security, make trustless agreements through Smart Contract, make compliance easier and much more.

Moreover, thanks to the innovative nature of the blockchain, the ways in which new financial items can interact with each other can potentially lead to completely new types of financial services.

Advantages of the blockchain for the banking system

The blockchain offers different advantages that can truly help the banking system become more trustless and decentralized. Here are the main benefits the blockchain can provide to our financial system.

- **Security**. Blockchain-based architecture eliminates individual error points and reduces the need to deliver data into the hands of intermediaries.

- **Transparency**. The blockchain standardizes shared processes and creates a single shared source of truth for all network participants.

- **Trust**. Transparent registers allow different parts to collaborate and make agreements easier.
- **Programmability**. The blockchain allows reliable automation of commercial processes through the creation and execution of smart contracts.

- **Privacy**. Privacy Technologies made possible from BlockChain allow selective sharing of data between companies.

- **Performance**. Networks are designed to support a large number of transactions, at the same time supporting interoperability between different chains, thus creating an interconnected blockchain network.

Rapid transfer of funds using the blockchain

Sending money into the current banking system can be a rather long process, can impose various commissions for banks and customers and can request additional checks and administration. In the instant connectivity era, the traditional banking system failed to keep up with the rest of technological developments.

Blockchain technology offers a faster payment method and with lower commissions, available at any time, without borders and with the same security guarantees that the traditional system can offer.

Asset tokenization on the blockchain

Buying and selling titles and other assets, such as actions, bonds, commodity, currencies and derivatives, requires a complex and coordinated effort between banks, brokers, compensation agencies and exchange platforms. This process should not only be efficient, but accurate as well. The added complexity directly corresponds to the increase in times and costs.

Blockchain technology simplifies this process by providing a basic technological level that makes tokenization of any type of asset possible. Given that much of the financial assets is bought and sold digitally through online brokers, the tokenization on the blockchain seems to be a convenient solution for all interested parties.

Some innovative blockchain companies are looking for physical asset tokenization, such as real estate, works of art and raw materials. This would make the transfer of the asset property with a convenient and economical process in the real world. Furthermore, it would offer new opportunities for investors with a limited capital, allowing them to buy a fractional property of expensive assets - investment products that could not be accessed before.

Loan grant using the blockchain

Banks and other loan companies have monopolized the credit sector, thus managing to offer loans with relatively high interest rates and limit access to capital based on credit scores. This makes the process of concession of long and expensive loans. While banks have the advantage, the economy depends on the supply by the banks of the funds necessary for high-cost products, such as cars and houses.

Blockchain technology allows anyone in the world to participate in a new type of loan ecosystem, which is part of the movement often defined as decentralized finance (DEFI). To create a more accessible financial system, the DEFI aims to develop and offer all financial applications on the blockchain.

Peer-to-peer money loans, allowed by the blockChain, allow everyone to lend and borrow in a simple, safe and inexpensive way, without arbitrary restrictions. With a more competitive loan sector, banks will be forced to offer better terms to their customers.

The impact of the blockchain on global trade

Participation in international trade is extremely evident due to a large number of international standards and regulations imposed on importers and exporters. Keeping track of goods and moving them through each phase still requires manual processes, full of documentation and handwritten records.

Blockchain technology allows participants from commercial finance to provide a higher level of transparency thanks to a shared register that accurately monitors moving goods in the globe. Simplifying and optimizing the complex world of commercial finance, blockchain technology allows importers, exporters and other companies to save large amounts of time and money.

Safe agreements via smart contract

Contracts exist to protect people and businesses when they enter into agreements, but this protection has a high cost. Due to the complex nature of contracts, the process necessary to create one requires a lot of manual work by legal experts.

Smart contracts allow the automation of the agreements through deterministic code testing tampering running on the BlockChain. Money can remain safe at ESCROW and is released only when certain conditions of the agreement have been met.

Smart contracts substantially reduce the element of trust necessary to reach an agreement, minimizing the risks linked to financial agreements and the chances of ending up in court.

Integrity and security of data enabled by the blockchain

The sharing of data with trusted imminators always involves the risk that the data is compromised. Furthermore, many financial institutions still use paper-based storage methods, which significantly increases accounting costs.

BlockChain technology enables optimized processes that automate verification and data recording, digitize KYC / AML data and transaction history, and makes real-time authentication of financial documents possible. This helps reduce operational risks, the risk of fraud, and reduces costs related to data management for financial institutions.

The banking and financial sector is one of the main sectors that will be revolutionized by the blockchain. The potential cases of use are numerous, from real-time transactions to asset tokenization, loans, simpler international trade, safer digital agreements and much more.

The resolution of all the technological and regulatory difficulties that hinder the potential of this new financial infrastructure seems to be just a matter of time. A bank and financial system based on a trustless, transparent and borderless base level is the most effective tool for creating a more open and interconnected economy.

Chapter 28

Bitcoin Blockchain and Safety

In this book we have often mentioned that the blockchain is an incredible safe and secure technology to store transactions. But what makes it so secure? Well, in this chapter we are going to dive deeper into this aspect.

Blockchain are protected through a variety of mechanisms, including advanced cryptographic techniques and behavioral and decision-making mathematical models. Blockchain technology is the structure below most of the cryptocurrency systems and is what prevents duplication or destruction of this type of digital money.

The use of blockchain technology is currently under development in other contexts in which immutability and data security are very valuable. Some examples include the registration and monitoring of beneficial donations, medical databases, and management of logistics chains.

However, blockchain security is certainly not a simple topic. Therefore, it is important to understand the concepts and basic mechanisms that give solid protection to these innovative systems.

The concepts of immutability and consensus

Although there are many elements that contribute to the security associated with blockchain, two of the most important are the concepts of consensus and immutability. The consensus refers to the capacity of the nodes within a distributed network blockchain to agree on the actual state of the network and on the validity of the transactions. Generally, the process to achieve consensus depends on the so-called consent algorithms.

Immutability, on the other hand, refers to the ability of the blockchain to prevent alteration of those transactions that have already been confirmed. Although these transactions are often linked to the transfer of cryptocurrencies, they can also refer to the registry of other forms of digital data.

Combined, consensus and immutability provide data security structure in the blockchain network. While the consensus algorithms guarantee that the rules of the system are followed and that all the parties involved agree on the current state of the network - immutability guarantees the integrity of data and transaction records after each new data block is confirmed as valid.

The role of encryption in the safety of Blockchain

Blockchains make extensive use of encryption to get their data security. A cryptographic function that takes

on extreme importance in this context is hashing. Hashing is a process in which a known algorithm as a hash function receives a data input (of any size) and returns a determined output that contains a fixed length value.
Regardless of the dimensions of the input, the output always has the same length. If the input is changed, the output will be completely different. However, if the input does not change, the resulting hash will always be the same - no matter how many times the hash function is performed.
Inside blockchain, these output values, known as hashes, are used as unique identifiers for data blocks. The hash of each block is generated in relation to the previous block hash, a factor that connects the blocks together, thus forming a chain. Furthermore, the block hash depends on the data contained within it, so any changes to the data would also require the modification of the block hash.

As a result, each block hash is generated based on both the data contained within it and on the previous block hash. These hash identifiers play a fundamental role in

ensuring the safety and immutability of the blockchain.
Hashing is also exploited in the consent algorithms used to validate transactions. In the Bitcoin Blockchain, for example, the Proof of Work (POW) algorithm used to reach consensus and for mining new units exploits a hash function called SHA-256. As the name suggests, SHA-256 transforms the input data into a 256-bit long hash or 64 characters.

In addition to providing protection for transactions stored on the registers, encryption is also used to guarantee the safety of the wallets used to store the tokens. The pair of public and private keys that allow users to receive and send payments is created through the use of asymmetrical or public key cryptography. Private keys are used to generate digital signatures for transactions, allowing you to authenticate the property of transferring tnits.
It is not necessary to go down to the details for the purpose of this chapter, it is enough to know that the nature of asymmetrical encryption prevents anyone except for the owner of the private key to access the funds preserved in a cryptocurrency wallet, thus

maintaining such funds safe until when the owner decides to spend them (as long as the private key is not shared or compromised).

Crypto Economy

In addition to encryption, a relatively new concept known as crypt economics plays a role in maintaining the security of the blockchain network. It refers to the study field known as game theory, which mathematically formulates decision-making processes of rational actors in situations with predefined rules and rewards. While the traditional game theory can be applied to a wide range of cases, the crypto economy model specifically describes the behavior of nodes within distributed blockchain systems.

In short, the crypto economy is the study of the economic aspect of blockchain protocols and the possible results that their design could submit according to the behavior of the participants. Security through crypto economy is based on the notion that blockchain systems offer better incentives to nodes that honestly act instead of adopting malicious or incorrect behavior. Again, the proof of work consensus algorithm used in the mining of Bitcoin offers an excellent example of this incentive scheme.

When Satoshi Nakamoto created the structure for Bitcoin mining, the process was intentionally conceived as expensive in terms of resources. Due to its complexity and its computational needs, the mining process involves a considerable investment of time and money - regardless of where the mining node is located. As a result, this structure places a strong disincentive to malicious actions and remarkable incentives for honest mining activities. The dishonest or inefficient nodes are quickly expelled from the blockchain network, while honest and efficient miners have the potential to receive substantial rewards for blocks.

Similarly, this balance of risks and rewards also guarantees protection from potential attacks that aim to compromise consent by accumulating the majority of the Hash Rate of a blockchain network in the hands of a single group or entity. These attacks, known as 51 percent attack, could be extremely harmful if performed successfully. Due to the competitiveness of the mining proof of work and the size of the Bitcoin network, the probability that an attacker is able to get control of the majority of nodes is really minimal.

Furthermore, the cost of the computational power necessary to obtain 51 percent of the control of a huge blockchain network would be astronomical, placing an immediate disincentive to such a huge investment for a potential small reward. As long as the cost linked to establishing a majority of dishonest nodes remains prohibitive and there are better incentives for honest activity, the system will be able to thrive without significant disorders. It should be emphasized that smaller blockchain networks are undoubtedly susceptible to the attacks described above, given that the total hash rate dedicated to these systems is considerably lower than that of bitcoin.

Through the combined use of game theory and encryption, blockchains are able to reach high levels of security as distributed systems. However, as for almost all systems, it is essential that these two fields of knowledge are adequately applied. An accurate balance between decentralization and safety is vital for the development of a reliable and effective network.

As the cases of use of blockchain continue to evolve, even security systems will develop to meet the needs of various applications. Private blockchain currently under development for commercial enterprises, for example, make greater reliance on safety through access control instead of based on the mechanisms of game theory that are essential for the security of many public blockchains.

Chapter 29

The 2021 Bull Market

Market trends are among the most fundamental aspects of the financial markets. We can define a market trend as the general direction in which an asset or market moves. For this reason, market trends are closely monitored by technical analysts and fundamental analysts.

Bull markets tend to be relatively easy to exploit, as they allow for the use of the simplest trading and investment strategies. Even inexperienced investors could perform well in really favorable bull market conditions. However, it remains crucial to understand that markets move in cycles.

So what should you know about bull markets? How do investors take advantage of bull markets? You can find the answers in this chapter.

What is a bull market?

A bull market (or bull run) is the scenario in a financial market where prices are rising. The term bull market is often used in the context of the stock market. However, it can be used in any financial market - including Forex, bonds, commodities, real estate, and cryptocurrencies. Furthermore, the expression bull market could also refer to a specific asset such as Bitcoin or Ethereum. It could describe a sector, such as utility tokens, privacy coins, or biotech stocks.

You may have already heard Wall Street traders use the terms "bullish" and "bearish”. When an investor says he is bullish in a market, it means that he expects prices to rise. When bearish, he predicts a drop in prices.

Often being bullish can mean having a long position in the market, but this is not necessarily the case. A bullish condition may not present a long opportunity at the moment but simply indicates that prices are rising or are expected to rise.

It is also important to highlight the fact that a bull market does not mean that prices do not fall or fluctuate. For this reason it is more reasonable to consider bull markets over longer time frames. In this sense, bull markets will include periods of decline or consolidation without invalidating the overall market trend. Take a look at the Bitcoin chart below. Despite periods of decline, and some violent market crashes, it has been in an overall bullish trend since its inception.

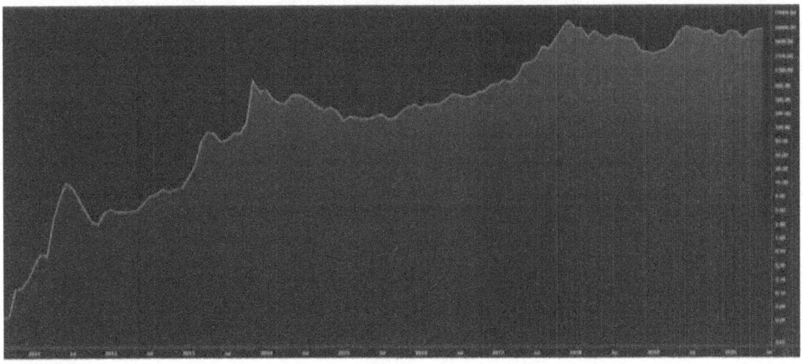

In this perspective, the definition of a bull market depends on the time periods that are taken into consideration. Generally, when we use the term bull market we are talking about a time span of months or years. As with other techniques used in market analysis, trends observed over longer periods tend to have more value than trends over shorter periods.

Thus, in a bull market over extended periods there may be prolonged phases of decline. These countertrend price movements are known for their particular volatility - although this can vary a lot from asset to asset.

Examples of a bull market

Some of the best-known examples of bull markets come from the stock market. We are talking about scenarios in which the prices of stocks and market indexes (such as the Nasdaq 100) are constantly increasing.

Taking the global economy into consideration, we know it fluctuates between bull and bear markets.

These market cycles can last for years or even decades. Some argue that the bull market that began following the 2008 financial crisis and ended due to the coronavirus pandemic was the "longest bull market in history." The validity of this claim is uncertain - as we said, bull markets over longer periods of time can be a matter of point of view.

Anyway, let's take a look at the long-term performance of the Dow Jones Industrial Average (DJIA). We can see that it is basically in a century-long bull market. Of course, there are periods of decline that can last for years, as in the case of 1929 or 2008, but the overall trend is still heading upwards.

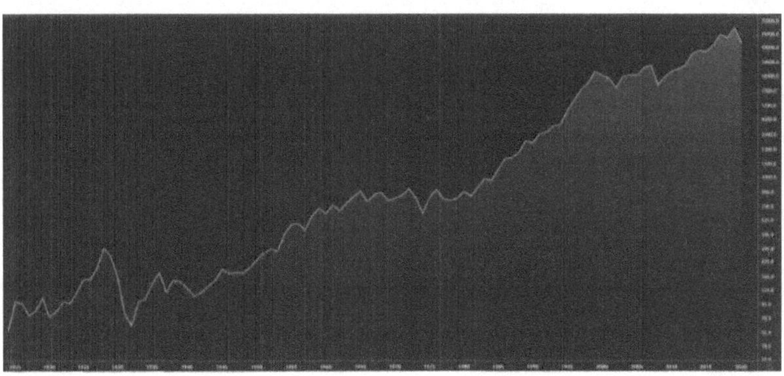

Some argue that we could see a similar trend in Bitcoin, but we can't say for sure when Bitcoin will face a multi-year bear market. Importantly, most other cryptocurrencies will likely never experience such appreciation, so be very careful what you invest in.

Bull market vs. bear market

These are opposite concepts, so the difference isn't very hard to guess. In a bull market, prices continually rise, while in a bear market, prices continually fall.

This also results in differences on the best methods for investing in the two conditions. In a bull market, investors will generally want to be long, while in a bear market they will want to be short or out of the market sitting on cash.

In some cases, even sitting on cash (or stablecoins) can mean being short on the market, as this means expecting prices to drop. The main difference is that holding the funds in cash is more about preserving capital, while a short position is meant to gain on falling asset prices. However, if you sell an asset with the intention of buying it back at a lower price, you are essentially in a short position - even if you are not directly profiting from the decline.

Another element to consider are fees. Staying in stablecoin is unlikely to lead to fees, as there are usually no costs associated with custody. Conversely, many short positions will require a financing fee or interest rate to ensure they are opened. As such, quarterly futures may be ideal for long-term short positions, as they do not charge funding fees.

How investors can benefit from bull markets

The central idea in bull market investing is relatively simple. Prices are going up, so opening long and buying corrections is generally a reasonable strategy. For this reason the buy and hold strategy and dollar cost averaging plan are generally suitable for long-term bull markets.

There is a saying that goes: "The trend is your friend, until it isn't anymore." This simply means that it makes sense to trade in the direction of the market trend. At the same time, no trend will last forever, and the same strategy may not perform well in other parts of a market cycle. The only certainty is the fact that markets can and will change. As we have seen for the COVID-19 pandemic, multi-year bull markets can be wiped out in a matter of weeks.

Of course, most investors will be bullish in a bull market. It makes sense as prices are rising, so overall sentiment should be bullish as well. However, even during a bull market, some investors will be bearish. If their investing strategy allows it, they may also be successful with short-term bearish trades.

Hence, some investors will try to open short on recent highs in a bull market. However, we are talking about advanced strategies that are generally more suited to professional investors. For less experienced investors, it usually makes more sense to trade following the market trend. Many investors get trapped when they try to make money shorting bull markets. After all, facing a raging bull can be a dangerous.

Chapter 30

Earning Passive Income on Bitcoin

We would like to end this book with a chapter dedicated to how you can use the bitcoins you bought to earn passive income. This is a great strategy if combined with the dollar cost averaging technique we have explained in a previous chapter. Before explaining to you how you can do this, it is important to know that it involves a third party company, called Blockfi. If you have read the entire book you know how much it is important to have full control of your private keys when you own cryptocurrencies. Blockfi is the only crypto related company we trust, as they have proven to be transparent and give regular proof of ownership of the funds. They have an affiliate program as well, but we will not share with you our affiliate link, because we do not want you to think we have an interest in recommending you this company.

Now that we have cleared this out, let's dive deeper into what Blockfi is and why it is an amazing company to earn interest on your bitcoins.

Blockfi is a cryptographic asset management platform that offers its users the opportunity to earn interests on their tokens. It offers loans in cryptocurrencies, StableCoin and USD to companies and organizations that try to monetize their resources.

This is perhaps the easiest way to make your cryptocurrencies generate passive income on the Blockfi platform. Once an account is opened you can deposit and start earning compound interests from day one.

You can create an Interest blockfish account by visiting the Blockfi website and to do so you must be at least eighteen. You have to go through a KYC process, where you have to upload a clear photo of your identity card. If all the details are correct, your account is approved in a few minutes. If your account has not been approved within 48 hours, you can write to onboarding@blockfi.com to get assistance and complete the verification process. For business accounts, you will need to send the identification information of managers and owners of your company's shares. Blockfi also offers promotions to attract customers and currently offers a registration bonus up to $250 with a deposit of at least $25 or higher. As we said you are asked to complete your KYC precisely because this helps the Blockfield Organization to prevent money laundering activities and other similar illicit practices.

The Blockfi interest account provides interests on deposits on the first working day of each month. A minimum balance is not required to earn interests. If you don't have some of the coins supported by the platform, you can transfer USD or EUR directly into your Blockfi interest account. Traditional FIAT money will be converted into any of the coins available. Rates may vary taking into account different factors, but they will provide you with information in advance about this. Furthermore, interest rates change once every two or three months compared to other platforms that change the rates on a weekly basis. Therefore, Blockfi provides rather constant earnings over time.

Blockfi also offers some flexibility in payments. If you are depositing your funds in a particular form of cryptocurrency, you can earn interest in the cryptocurrency of your choice. For example, if you have deposited BTC, you can earn in the form of BTC, ETH, LTC, USDC or USDT. You need to change this information at least two working days before the last working day of the month, so that the choice is respected with the right timing. Otherwise, if you don't, you will earn interest on the type of cryptocurrency you have originally deposited.

Blockfi also provides monthly statements that indicate the funds you give, the interest you have earned and the interests you can earn next month. Blockfi will send you monthly statements by email and you can also download them in PDF format directly from the platform. You can also download the transaction history in CSV file format in the appropriate section of your personal account. Furthermore, you can also filter transactions in a specific date range and download the report.

Blockfi generates interest by providing its funds to trusted companies and institutional borrowers, purchasing ETFs and other financial securities. An in-depth credit analysis is performed before lending money to anyone. You can also close your account whenever you prefer. If your portfolio has cryptocurrencies, you can transfer them to other accounts along with the related accrued interests. If you do not deposit any amount within sixty days from the opening of your account, it will be automatically closed by the system.

Cryptographic loans

The minimum loan amount is $10,000 and you can deposit Bitcoin, Ethereum or Litecoin as collateral. Money is then transferred to the customer account in dollars. Blockfi promotes this service as an ideal way to finance purchases of considerable entities, such as properties, cars, holidays and the like, or as an opportunity to diversify your financial portfolio.

How to use the blockfi trading platform

Blockfi users can also deposit funds on the platform and use them to buy more cryptocurrencies or stableCoin.

Blockfi has its own Exchange, which is available to all its users with a personal account. This allows investors on the platform to switch from one cryptocurrency to another in an intuitive way.
The best part is that you still earn compound interests while you trade.

To register for a Blockfi account, follow these simple steps:

- Visit the Blockfi website and create an account;

- Complete the email verification and access your account;
- Add funds to the account via the user's dashboard;
- Click "Exchange" in the Navigation Panel located at the top;
- Select the cryptocurrency you want to exchange;
- Enter the amount you want to buy;
- Review the order details and click Enter to finalize the transaction.

Blockfi introduced a new feature that allows users to send cash deposits by bank transfer to the platform. This involves Fiat currency transmission to buy stablecoins directly on the platform. The process is rather easy for beginners who have never bought Bitcoin before. They can register with Blockfi, deposit traditional currencies by bank transfer and receive up to 8.6% in a Blockfi interest account. USD dollar deposits are automatically exchanged in Gemini Dollars (GUS) which can then be converted into Bitcoin, Ethereum, Litecoin and USDC using the Blockfi trading platform.

To buy stablecoins using USD with Blockfi, follow these steps:

- Access your BlockFlen account.
- Click "Deposit" in the top navigation bar
- Select "USD (bank transfer)" as a deposit currency.
- Select "Bank transfer" as a payment method
- Enter your details and send your bank transfer to Blockfi

The Blockfi team

The company was founded in 2017 and is based in New Jersey. Its co-founders are Zac Prince and Flori Marquez, who serve respectively as CEO and SVP of operations. Prince has a degree in International Business at Texas State University and a technology background, having been vice-president of business development at Orchard Platform and sales manager at Sociomantic Labs. Marquez, graduated from Cornell and is one of the rising stars in the banking and financial sector. Rene Van Kesteren is Chief Risk

Officer and spent thirteen years at Bank of America Merrill Lynch before joining Blockfi. The other main member of the executive group is the CTO Mahesh Paolini-Subramanya, who worked in the technological sector since he graduated from the University of Notre Dame at the end of the 1980s.

The rest of the managerial team has a similar mix of experience in Fintech and traditional finance, while the company as a whole employs 65 people distributed in four offices between New Jersey, New York, Argentina and Poland.

One of the most reliable metrics when evaluating a relatively new company is its list of initial investors. Blockfi has impressive support in this field, including Akuna Capital caliber actors, coellid ventures, Galaxy Digital Ventures and the Winklevoss twins.

How Blockfish works

If you are trying to earn interest, get a loan or trading, you can only do it with Bitcoin, Ethereum or Litecoin.

When it comes to loans, you need more capital to be deposited as a guarantee to benefit from the minimum loan of $10,000. The maximum loan to value ratio (LTV) is 50%, with additional rates available.

It is worth discussing exactly how these loans are structured.

The requests are processed rapidly and, if you apply in a working day, you can wait for a decision from Blockfi in about two hours. Blockfi uses several factors to calculate interest rates, including the amount of the loan, location and particular warranty provided. This is undoubtedly of great attraction for those in the cryptocurrency space that are trying to get rid of some restrictions that traditional finance puts in place. Obviously, if the value of the collateral has increased in that time frame, you may be able to recover some of the expenses commissions. Conversely, if the collateral value suddenly decreases, you may need to provide additional funds or pay the loan balance.

Who can use blockfi?

The company identified "three main types of organizations" that use the services provided:

- **Traders and investment funds.** Essentially those looking for arbitrage opportunities that need to borrow cryptocurrencies to close the price spreads between different markets. "Margin" traders may also have to contract loans to cover the costs of their trading strategies

- **"Over the Counter" market operators (OTC)**. These are buyers and sellers wishing to do business away from public exchanges, which often have high commissions.

- **Companies that need liquidity in cryptocurrencies.** They may want to maintain most of their resources in Cold Wallets but they still need liquidity to provide ordinary operations of their customers. The Crypto ATMs can be quoted as an example.

Blockfi commissions

Users who create a Blockfi interest account will then be subject to limits and withdrawal commissions as follows:

- Bitcoin: commission of 0.0025 BTC and 100 per week limit
- Ethereum: commission of 0.0015 ETH and $5K limit per week
- Litecoin: commission of 0.0025 LTC and limit of $10,000 per week
- Stablecoins: commission of $0.25 USD and $1 million limit per week

There is no minimum balance to earn interests with blockfi.

You can also enjoy a free withdrawal of cryptocurrencies and stablecoins every month and you can collect it at any time you prefer. Each free withdrawal applies for a single cryptocurrency every month. After making a request, your cryptocurrency will first be transferred to Blockfi Trading LLC and later at the requested address. If you want to make an additional withdrawal, you will be charged the relevant commission as we have listed before.

Blockfi and safety

The main custody Exchange of Blockfi is Gemini, (of the famous Winklevoss brothers) which has recently completed a "SoC 2" compliance conformity, which made it the first exchange of cryptocurrencies to achieve this level of security. The exchange is regulated by the Department of Financial Services of the New York State (NYDFS) and retains 95% of its resources in a Cold Wallet. According to the website, in fact, even the same twins would not be able to transfer cryptocurrencies contained in that wallet without permission. In short, Gemini's security protocols are no second to anyone and the possibilities that funds are stolen are extremely low. Even if such a violation occurs, all the funds are insured by AON and any losses would be offset.

Higher security systems

In addition to the safety of Gemini, Blockfi uses a range of features to keep the accounts of its customers safe. Two-factor authentication is active and all passwords, personal and sensitive information is encrypted. The platform also allows users to practice the "AllowListing" (otherwise known as Whitelisting) on their accounts, so the funds can be collected only to certain addresses, that needs to be specified and approved.

It would take an immensely sophisticated attack to extract funds from Blockfi and even in that case the insurance would cover any loss. No customer deposit has been stolen and if an account is compromised, it would be immediately frozen for a week and a video conferencing would be conducted with the customer concerned to confirm its identity. You can then run the steps to change passwords and email addresses to ensure that the customer can resume control of your personal account.

Institutional Blockfi services

Blockfi provides institutional services such as personalized loans also in the form of stablecoins, cryptocurrency and fiat currencies such as USD. Blockfi supports quick onboarding i.e. a rapid execution of exchanges with its company level reporting. You will be followed step by step in the entire loan creation process. For more details, you can contact the team by filling out a special request form provided by the site.

In the arena of cryptocurrency-based loans and encryption accounts, Blockfi is certainly well positioned among the first 3 platforms available in the market. The platform constantly innovates and always adds new features. Considering the high interest rate it offers right now and the fact that it has been in business for over 4 years, we can advise you to put a portion of your holdings into a Blockfi interest account.

Conclusion

Congratulations on making it to the end of this book, we hope you found some useful insights to take your cryptocurrency trading skills to the next level. As you should know by now, the world of Bitcoin is extremely complicated and there is a new "opportunity" every way you look. However, our experience tells us that only by taking things seriously and having a proper plan you can develop your investing skills to the point that you can actually accumulate wealth.

Our final advice is to stay away from the shining objects that the world of cryptocurrencies offers you every day. Simply dollar cost average into Bitcoin and study the world of cryptocurrencies in depth. After you have sufficient knowledge on what you are talking about, you can go ahead and invest into other cryptocurrencies. Analyze your results, improve your money management skills and become the master of your emotions.

As you can see, there are no shortcuts you can take. Easy money does not exist. What exists is the possibility to start from zero and work your way up to become a professional Bitcoin investor. The journey might be difficult, but it is certainly worth it.

www.ingramcontent.com/pod-product-compliance
Lightning Source LLC
Chambersburg PA
CBHW050827150926
51501CB00040B/445